The Biddle Boys and Mrs. Soffel. The Great Pittsburg Tragedy and Romance

Arthur Forrest

The Biddle Boys and Mrs. Soffel. The Great Pittsburg Tragedy and Romance
Trial of The Biddle Boys and Mrs. Soffel
Arthur Forrest
HAR00416
Monograph
Harvard Law School Library
Philadelphia, Pa.: Royal Publishing Company, 630 Locust Street, 1902

The Making of Modern Law collection of legal archives constitutes a genuine revolution in historical legal research because it opens up a wealth of rare and previously inaccessible sources in legal, constitutional, administrative, political, cultural, intellectual, and social history. This unique collection consists of three extensive archives that provide insight into more than 300 years of American and British history. These collections include:

Legal Treatises, 1800-1926: over 20,000 legal treatises provide a comprehensive collection in legal history, business and economics, politics and government.

Trials, 1600-1926: nearly 10,000 titles reveal the drama of famous, infamous, and obscure courtroom cases in America and the British Empire across three centuries.

Primary Sources, 1620-1926: includes reports, statutes and regulations in American history, including early state codes, municipal ordinances, constitutional conventions and compilations, and law dictionaries.

These archives provide a unique research tool for tracking the development of our modern legal system and how it has affected our culture, government, business – nearly every aspect of our everyday life. For the first time, these high-quality digital scans of original works are available via print-on-demand, making them readily accessible to libraries, students, independent scholars, and readers of all ages.

old books. new life.

The BiblioLife Network

This project was made possible in part by the BiblioLife Network (BLN), a project aimed at addressing some of the huge challenges facing book preservationists around the world. The BLN includes libraries, library networks, archives, subject matter experts, online communities and library service providers. We believe every book ever published should be available as a high-quality print reproduction; printed on-demand anywhere in the world. This insures the ongoing accessibility of the content and helps generate sustainable revenue for the libraries and organizations that work to preserve these important materials.

The following book is in the "public domain" and represents an authentic reproduction of the text as printed by the original publisher. While we have attempted to accurately maintain the integrity of the original work, there are sometimes problems with the original work or the micro-film from which the books were digitized. This can result in minor errors in reproduction. Possible imperfections include missing and blurred pages, poor pictures, markings and other reproduction issues beyond our control. Because this work is culturally important, we have made it available as part of our commitment to protecting, preserving, and promoting the world's literature.

GUIDE TO FOLD-OUTS MAPS and OVERSIZED IMAGES

The book you are reading was digitized from microfilm captured over the past thirty to forty years. Years after the creation of the original microfilm, the book was converted to digital files and made available in an online database.

In an online database, page images do not need to conform to the size restrictions found in a printed book. When converting these images back into a printed bound book, the page sizes are standardized in ways that maintain the detail of the original. For large images, such as fold-out maps, the original page image is split into two or more pages

Guidelines used to determine how to split the page image follows:

• Some images are split vertically; large images require vertical and horizontal splits.
• For horizontal splits, the content is split left to right.
• For vertical splits, the content is split from top to bottom.
• For both vertical and horizontal splits, the image is processed from top left to bottom right.

...THE...

BIDDLE BOYS

AND MRS. SOFFEL.

THE GREAT PITTSBURG TRAGEDY AND ROMANCE.

WITH FULL DESCRIPTION OF THEIR LIVES AND CRIMES.

——BY——

ARTHUR FORREST.

(JOURNALIST)

ILLUSTRATED.

ROYAL PUBLISHING COMPANY,
530 LOCUST STREET   PHILADELPHIA, PA.

PREFACE.

The presentation of this most thrilling narrative of crime, love, daring, adventure and tragedy is with the intent to portray fully, graphically and interestingly one of the most startling occurrences of modern history, and to perpetuate what was perhaps the most romantic and sensational tragedies this country has ever known Never before in the history of America has a prison warden's wife conspired with and assisted condemned convicts to escape, and then, to cap the climax, deserted husband, children, home, and position, to go with one of them — the man she had foolishly learned to love Her pity at first — worked upon no doubt by the clever convict as he perceived the impression he had made — soon grew into an insane passion of love, and she gave all any woman could give save her life, and she nearly gave that, too.

Whether the Biddles were guilty or innocent of the murder for which they were to have been hanged will never be known until that great day when all mankind shall appear before the Highest Judge for reward or punishment. They are dead, and even the merciless law should be satisfied. The hapless woman who sacrificed so much for them is recovering from the pistol-shot wound she received in the breast during the fusilade that preceded their capture, and when she has fully recovered she will be arraigned in Pittsburg to answer for the felony of assisting State convicts to escape Her punishment may be a term of years in the very cell from which she helped the man she loved and his brother to escape. The facts and details here chronicled are the fullest and most accurate, compiled by a well-known journalist who was present when the fatal finish on the snow-covered road took place, and who stood beside the Biddle boys when they breathed their last More thrillingly interesting scenes were never enacted in the drama of real life, and on these pages they will be found most faithfully portrayed.

THE AUTHOR.

ED. BIDDLE'S POEM.

Glorification of a Flower sent to His Prison Cell.

The following verses were written on the flyleaf of a volume of Longfellow's poems by Ed Biddle in the death cell of the Pittsburg Jail, and sent by him to the little daughter of the Rev F N. Foster, his former spiritual adviser   The gift was in recognition of a pretty flower the child had sent to him by one of the prison guards.

Just a little violet,
　From across the way,
Came to cheer a prisoner
　In his cell one day.

Just a little flower,
　Sent by loving hand;
Has a kindly meaning,
　That true hearts understand.

Just a little violet,
　Plucked with tender care;
God has smiled upon it,
　And the sender fair.

So now that little token,
　Wrapped tight in paper neat,
Rests quietly within a grave,
　O'er which a heart does beat.

MRS. SOFFEL.

A TRAGIC ROMANCE.

--------- •

Unparalleled in the History of the World, is this Wonderful Life Story of Love and Death.

The story of the Biddle boys and Mrs Soffel belongs to another age than that in which we are living today. It has all the flavor of the old border romance, where "all for love and the world well lost" was a good enough code of morals, and when knightly quality was a cloak in which many a bold outlaw posed as a hero.

But in this Twentieth Century the story, scattered broadcast by the wires instead of sung by some wandering minstrel, seems almost incredible as the tale of a woman who gives her heart to a convicted murderer, and, throwing honor and duty to the winds, sets him free of prison bars, and of a man who, crime-stained as he was, refused to buy safety by deserting the woman who loved him!

A few days ago, in the old gray Jail of Pittsburg City, the Biddle brothers, condemned to death for murder, were counting the last days of their little span of existence They were bad men They had taken what they wanted of life with strong hands, and their careers were black with unnumbered robberies, and stained red with blood. But now they had come

7

to the end. Prison walls shut them in, and from their prison windows they saw no hope — only the grim walls of the warden's house

Then, one day, at a window, they saw a woman's face It was Warden Soffel's wife Ed smiled, and for the first time hope seemed to beckon to him again. By and by Mrs Soffel came to the jail, idly curious to see the noted criminals, whose daring robberies and nervy murders had made them noted through all the countryside

Ed began to talk to her, and found in her a ready listener Then she spoke to him of holy things, and brought him a Bible He professed to have been cheered and comforted and helped by its pasages, and

she got in the way of visiting him at the jail, bringing him reading matter, and delicacies from her own table.

Ed Biddle was a handsome man, and he had that fascination so many such men have for women Somewhere he had picked up a smattering of education He had a pretty knack of versifying, and could draw flowers so perfectly you could fancy you smelled their perfume   Perhaps it was this strange blending of ferocity and force and gentleness of the murderer and poet that captured the fancy of the simple woman   Anyway, as so many other women had done before her, she set her heart upon him

It was nothing to her that she had husband and children   She lived only for the few minutes daily when her sweetheart whispered passionate words of devotion to her through the iron-barred doorway, or signalled tender messages by love's telegraphy from his window to hers

There has been no stranger human document than this story, but it belongs to the past — to the days of the swashbuckling hero in velvet doublet and beplumed hat, not to this prosaic, conventional age, that prides itself upon having gotten away from the primitive emotions, and does not take romance into account when judging crime

HISTORY OF THE BIDDLES.

Canadians by Birth, they were the Offspring of Drunken and Worthless Parents.

The Biddle boys were Canadians by birth, having first seen the light of day in the village of Amherstburg, in the Province of Ontario, eighteen miles west of Windsor. Their father was George Biddle, a former resident of New York State, who moved to Canada when the Civil War broke out in order to evade conscription. There were eight children in the family— Edward and John, who figured in this most tragic occurrence, Patrick, who is now serving a term in the Pennsylvania Penitentiary for burglary, Harry, now living in Pittsburg, and two other sons and daughters who are now living somewhere in the Fa West. The father was shiftless, and the boys were given no education. They were left largely to shift for themselves, and a drunken father and worthless mother, living in a hand-to-mouth manner that was simply an existence, soon had its pernicious effect on them, and they grew up in idleness and dissipation, with no idea of ever earning their own livings by honest toiling. After several escapades with the Ontario police, they were arrested at an early age for holding up and robbing an old man who lived near where they did, and were sentenced to prison. While in the rickety little county jail they made their escape and fled to Chicago, where under other names they began a new career of crime. There they associated with the lowest classes of men and women, and their lives very quickly became those of desperadoes After a year or two of wild crime and dissipation they were arrested for burglarizing a jewelry store, and sent to the Juliet Penitentiary Owing to their youth, however, the judge was lenient and gave them only a short sentence After it expired they came out worse men than ever, and filled with but one desire — to live in ease and luxury without working They perpetrated petty swindles of all sorts and committed small thefts when they got the chance They went about the suburbs bilking farmers and others with gambling games, and for a while followed the county fairs with a gang of other " grafters " whose only object was to secure money — now, it mattered not At last things went against them in Chicago, and the police were again on their trail Naturally, they fled, and Fate directed their steps to Pittsburg They stayed there but a few days — long enough to rob an old jeweler of his stock of diamonds valued at several thousand dollars, and then they fled to Cincinnati, where they spent a few months of riotous living. When the proceeds of the robbery were gone they went to Cleveland and started a new career of crime A series of the most daring burglaries that were ever heard of startled that city, and it was had the place in a state of terror People were held up and robbed in broad daylight, and robbed of their watches, money or valuables The pockets of street-car conductors were picked on the crowded cars Ed Biddle held a woman in bed at the point of a pistol while his brother robbed the house, and even tore a gold chain bracelet off her arm. The cashier of a bank, who was approached by the well-dressed and gentlemanly Ed, pretending he wanted to make a deposit, was suddenly confronted with a pistol and ordered to hand over the bundle of bank notes which lay in front of him. To save his life he did so, and with over seven thousand dollars the daring robbers fled. The finale to the reign of terror they had inaugurated in Cleveland resulted in their subsequent arrest after a desperate battle with the police, and they were sentenced to a term in the Ohio Penitentiary. Staunch friends they had made prior to their arrest prevailed upon the Governor to pardon them, and unwisely he did so. They then went to Erie, Pa., where they played upon the sympathies of the people until they got a foothold, and then commenced another series of burglaries. After many successful hauls the Biddles were again the objects of official pursuit, an disappeared. They turned up at Pittsburg next, and made things lively for a while in the burglary line. They took with them two women — Jennie Zebers and Jessie Bodine — and it is said the women assisted them in the burglaries. If a house was to be robbed, one of them applied for a position as a domestic, and late at night, or when the family was absent, admitted her lover, and the house was looted. During the police investigation that followed she pluckily remained in service, and thus threw off suspicion. If a man was to be held up, the women lured him to some out-of-the-way place, and he was an easy victim. The old badger game, in which the "good thing" was lured to a room by a woman whose supposed husband turned up a few moments after their arrival and demanded his money, was also resorted to, and many fell easy prey. But at last all these games played out, and a bold stroke was decided upon.

STORY OF THE CRIME,

The Foul Murder for which the Biddle Boys Paid
Their Lives. A Woman is Alleged to have
Fired the Fatal Shot that Killed
Grocer Kahney.

The crime for which the Biddle boys paid their lives
was in all probability not committed by them, but they
were accessories and, therefore, equally guilty under
the law

On the outskirts of Pittsburg, in an isolated locality,
there lived an old grocer, named George Kahney, who,
it was reported, had amassed quite a fortune   He was
an eccentric old man, and did not believe in putting
money in bank   Whatever he had he always kept
about him, and it was rumored had a large amount
of ready cash stowed away in his house   He was of
reticent disposition, and said nothing about his affairs
to anyone   The Biddles learned of his supposed
wealth, and a robbery was decided upon   Walter
Dorman, a former lover of the Bodine woman, was
the man who first suggested the robbery and told of
the old grocer's hidden treasure   Calmly the plans
were made for the robbery, and every detail figured
out. It was agreed Jessie Bodine should go to the
store and make a trifling purchase, after which she

was to engage the old man in conversation and get him interested, while others entered the house from the rear and ransacked it for his hidden gold. Their plans were well laid, and Jennie Zebers decided she would dress as a man and, with a mask on her face, assist in the burglary. She was given a pistol, with which to intimidate anyone who might confront her, but in his dying confession Ed Biddle said she killed the victim, although he had no idea she would use the weapon. After long deliberation, the night of April 12, 1901, was selected as that on which Kahney was to be robbed, and after dark Ed and Jack Biddle, Walter Dorman and the two women went to his place armed to the teeth. It was a wild, stormy night, and but few persons were around. The lights shone brightly from the windows of the old grocer's shop, and he busied himself behind the counter, setting things to rights, as, owing to the weather, there were no customers. All this favored the robbers' ends, and shortly before 10 o'clock the Bodine woman was sent ahead and entered the shop. She bought some trifling article, and began a conversation with the old grocer. It had been a dull evening with him, and he was glad of a chat with the comely young woman. She talked to him about everything she could think of, and meanwhile her partners in crime were breaking their way into the house from the rear. A pair of shutters on a rear window were forced, and one of the Biddle boys started to get in, but found the window too small to admit his body, and the Zebers woman, who was slender, was assisted in and told to unbolt the back door. This she did, and the ransacking of the house was in progress when the old man in the store heard a suspicious noise. "That sounds like someone in the

14

house," he said to the Bodine woman "Oh, no! it's nothing but the wind rattling the shutters," she replied, as she tried to throw him off suspicion. He, however, persisted there was someone in the house, and rushed to the door in the back of the store, which communicated with the house. At this juncture Jessie Bodine's nerve forsook her, and she fled into the street. The poor old man, little dreaming of the fate in store for him, rushed into the room and confronted Jennie Zebers She drew the pistol, with the idea of intimidating him, and a-second later fired With a bullet through his brain, the old man fell to the floor a corpse Horror-stricken at what she had done, she fled, and the others also left with her, without making any further attempt at robbery Hours later a passing policeman found the store open and unattended, and upon going into the back room to call the proprietor found him lying murdered on the floor, weltering in his life blood, which poured from a hole in his head. The officer gave the alarm, and the next day Pittsburg was horrified by the story of the foul murder No details were known, and there were no witnesses other than the criminals themselves, but the police somehow suspected the Biddles, whom they knew to be bad men, and on this suspicion went to work. They learned at their boarding-house they were out the night of the murder, and some other things which led them to follow up the trail. As their investigation progressed more and more circumstances were found which pointed to the suspects, and at last there was enough circumstantial evidence secured to arrest them. The whole party was surprised that night at their rooms Detective James Fitzpatrick, one of the most efficient and nervy of Pittsburg's police force, was in the lead of the officers, and broke into the rooms where the men and women were The instant the door opened the Biddles reached for their weapons, and someone — Ed Biddle, it is believed — fired a shot which struck Fitzpatrick in the breast and instantly killed him He fell dead to the floor, but there were others close behind him, and soon all hands were disarmed and under arrest

They were taken to jail, and there Dorman turned State's evidence and confessed all, after being promised immunity from punishment if he did so. He told all about the murder, but did not say who shot the grocer or the detective On these points he swore he did not know, and his evidence was more directly against the Biddle boys and tended to clear the women, he claiming they were duped into the job and knew nothing of what was to occur. On this testimony the Biddles were found guilty at their trial, and the women were acquitted They immediately left for parts unknown, and the Biddles were sentenced to death They were taken to the Pittsburg Jail, and it was intended to hang them February 24, as the Governor had set that date for their execution They remained in jail quietly awaiting the end, apparently, when Ed Biddle wrote an appeal to Governor Stone, asking him to change the date of execution. He begged he and his brother be not hanged together, and incidentally asked a little more time to prepare for the awful end This the Governor granted, and postponed the dates of the hangings until March, when Ed was to have been hanged on Wednesday and John on Friday of the second week. From that moment the doomed men had new hopes, and began preparing to cheat the gallows

THE BIDDLE BOYS' TRIAL.

Sensational Scenes in the Old Court House during the Trial of the Desperadoes and the Attention they Attracted.

There was something about the Biddle boys which attracted women. No one ever knew just what it was, but it had its effect — call it personal magnetism or what you like — and the courtroom during their trials was continually packed with women. Ed was a dashing fellow, while his brother looked far more the criminal that he was. Foolish women, fascinated by the glances of Ed, grew to believe him innocent, and took him flowers and dainties to the jail and court-room. The court was packed at each session and, shameful be it said, there were many prominent women in the courtroom daily who seemed more than pass-ingly interested in the dashing young criminals on trial. The attorney for their defense made an able plea for them, and resorted to every known hook and crook of the law to save their necks, but it was use-less. Their records were against them, and the jury readily believed all the grim old State's Attorney al-leged against them. It was clearly shown they were born criminals of the most dangerous class, and that they had deliberately planned the robbery which ended

MRS. SOFFEL.

in the murder of the old man For the women the
attorney for the defense made a most piteous plea,
pictured their youth, and how they had been led astray,
and vehemently declared they had nothing to do with
the foul crime other than to be the innocent victims of
others who lured them there While this was going
on the Biddles sat like statues, and the women were
convulsed with weeping They were young and good-
looking, and when the lawyer asked the jury if they
would consign those fair necks to the hangman's noose,
and the girls pleaded for their lives in a most piteous
manner, the jury, to a man, was soft-hearted enough
to believe they were guiltless of any intentional wrong
— and acquitted them Dorman's neck was, of course,
saved by the evidence he had given against the others,
and on the shoulders of the Biddle boys fell the burden
of the crime Quickly the jury declared them guilty
and that they should bear all the responsibility for the
death of Kahney They seemed dazed when the ver-
dict was rendered, and as they stood before the judge
and heard " and you shall be hanged by the neck until
you are both dead, and may God have mercy on your
souls," the morbid women with which the courtroom
was crowded burst into tears and wept until their wail
ings drowned the voice of the solemn-faced judge.
The courtroom was cleared, and the doomed men were
taken back to their cells From that moment they had
the sympathy of the women of Pittsburg, and from
that hour they began to foster it and make the most
of it. How well they did so their escape clearly shows.

ED. BIDDLE'S LOVE LETTER.

Last Missive of the Dead Bandit Written to the Warden's Wife and Found in Her Satchel.

A lost love letter from Ed Biddle to his prison sweetheart, Mrs Soffel, found in the snow near the bloody scene of their capture reveals the plot for the Biddle boys to escape from the Allegheny County Jail. The letter clearly shows the hazardous undertaking of the infatuated woman to secure the escape of the Biddles Since December 2, 1901, they had been making preparations to get away. The letter was evidently written before it was decided that Mrs Soffel would flee with the Biddles. The letter reads

My precious little darling. I guess I never will be able to kiss you good-bye. Oh, God, don't think that the blow is all on you. I love you, dearest baby, more than ever. Each minute today had been like an hour to me. You are dearer to me than my very life I will own up and tell you the truth

When I first started writing to you I did not love you. Now I have learned to love you better than my very life, and if I can't have you I want no one. In fact, I don't care for life at all. And I want to say is this: We were searched pretty close today, and those fellows would swear on a stack of Bibles 10 feet high

that we could not have had this stuff on us since
Saturday, so that you nearly clear yourself of all suspicion, unless the name of the fellow where you bought
the saws would come to the surface They never could
convict you, but some people might suspect you That
would cut no figure They could never prove it, to
save their lives

So now, baby darling, more precious to me than
ever, oh, God, ten times over, you are free to do as you
please It would be, of course, darling, safer for you
to stay at home until I could come and get you Of
course, it would be risking my freedom and life again
to do so, but I would risk more than that for you, if
possible You must not think I don't love you If
you have any reason, as I know you have, you must
not fail to see that I have risked all, that you have
given me right back, for you, to screen and protect
you Yes, darling, if I did not love you as dear as life
I would have left this place last Friday night So
darling, you know and must understand that your Ed
is true to his toe nails I never will do you wrong.

I know I have scolded you these last few days, but
it is only natural that I should feel bad to think that
another man's hands are on you after the way I love
you Good God, pet, if you love me as much as I do
you, you had better go Monday and take the chance
of everything coming out all right For if you love
me so, life for four or five months would be awful
to stand I want you as soon as I can get you If
you have $75 I will not stop one moment for money,
but fly right to you quick as I can No doubt my jaw
will swell and I ll suffer some, for it swells when I get
cold and I am sure to catch cold when I leave here

It would be much easier for us to get away if you

stayed at home, on account of the Warden, you know. In case you should not want to go, go to the postoffice at Homestead about March 18 and call for mail under the name of Mrs Charles McDonald You will get a letter telling you where I am, and how I am to get you I want you to suit yourself in this matter, my own darling, but I would rather you would go to-morrow, just as I have directed

Watch the papers close, and if you see they have traced us any part of the way, leave Toronto on the quiet and go to Montreal Leave letter in the Toronto office for me and as soon as you get settled in Montreal write me a letter to the postoffice there, all in signs, where you are Montreal is about 250 miles further north Keep low until I reach you

But it is not likely they will trace you if you are careful and do as I tell you in everything. You will be almost in your room before I am out and you need not go to the postoffice at all until I don't show up for eight or nine days You see, I'll get your letter as soon as I get there and will know where to find you right away, whether you are in Toronto or not

If you leave Toronto write me another letter and tell me, see? I'll get away all right, if the Warden is only asleep, and I think he will be, in case he does not find you have gone for good In that case he is likely to be prowling around, so do the best you can in regard to that, as it will be very important.

Oh, my darling, if I could only hold you in my arms once, press you to my heart, kiss your dear eyes, then you are mine forever, or until death claims you or me But in case it takes you first, it claims us both together, if you go and say to yourself " I want Ed, or none on this earth." Hide your morphine in the lining of your dress somewhere, so if you are searched, none could find it. And in case the worst comes to the worst, wait until you are alone, because if anyone knew you took it the doctors would pump it out with a stomach pump

My heart stops beating as I write these words, darling I only want to make you wise, as I can, along that line Death to you, my pet, would be worse than any form of death to me But I don't think it will ever come to that, pet I have all the confidence in the world in this game, but I don't want my only earthly love to live and curse me dead But if you will go, dear it will give me ten times the strength to handle these fellows If you stay at home, my heart grows faint at the idea of leaving you

My darling, if I ever get you once I will not leave you long and I'll be awful cautious and careful to see that I beat the suckers to a finish I could see despair written on your face, dearest heart, when you were refused admittance today I know it was not the thought of smallpox that did it

Now, pet, if you go Monday let me know as early as you can Come close to the window and say "I will go," for I can't see half you say if it is very light outside In the future when I can't see your sign I will put my hands around the bars When I can see your sign I will put my cleanest handkerchief around the bars If you go tomorrow I will then go tomorrow night, Monday night, and now, dear, be sure and don't keep me any longer, pet

You said, my little sweetheart, that instructions were not clear I don't understand that It don't do to have too much red tape about it You must think some yourself. It will be easy for you to go to Buffalo.

then to Niagara, which is 24 miles from Buffalo From
there take a bus and cross over the suspension bridge
into Canada You will meet custom house officers
when you reach the Canadian side Go to a bank, get
your American money changed to Canadian money,
then ask some boy or woman where the Grand Trunk
railway station is Get a ticket for Toronto

The reason I have to take so much caution is that
they will try to trace you to find me. They will say
right away, as soon as they come to a realization, that
you and I are together " Find her and you will get
the Biddle boys "

So I want you to smooth every track you make
Don't let them trace you from Pittsburg at all Change
your appearance so that no one will have seen you
if they are shown your photograph Do you understand, pet ? If they can't trace you to Buffalo you are
lost to them forever I may be with you in three or
four days, can't tell

You know what we have risked, and it would be
awful if it was all for nothing Don't go with that
friend of yours If you should I'll know it You
know what I have told you about that Don't think
I'll not know if you do If you've got the money I
don't want you to go near him any more You understand that now I don't even want you to go to him
for money if you haven't got it If you have five or
six rings that will be enough It won't cost over $10
fare

If you decide to stay at home, tell me Then you
will give me permission to go Everything has been
ready since Friday When you said you were going

to get the worst of it, that made me feel pretty bad, for I knew you meant it. I'm not made of that kind of metal, my dear one.

YOUR ED.

You will see by the papers, darling, in a day or two whether we have made it go or not. That will save you lots of suspense. I think you are writing to me and may want some things answered, so I'll save this sheet for that purpose. I guess you did not write anything. I could not see any of your signs this afternoon. You have been acting very strange of late. Always saying something that hurt my feelings. At least, you didn't seem to realize the seriousness of the situation.

Now, dear, I am going to go Monday night, just as sure as the sun shines in the heavens above. Tuesday morning I shall be a free man or a dead one. Bear that in mind. I can't understand you at all. Yes, dear, you can rely on my doing for once just what I said. I think that friend of yours has made you like him of late. If that is the case, just hang on to him and let me go peacefully. It is the best that way. And if you have kind of lost your love for me of late, it is too late to mend this affair. It has gone too far. I mean to be square with my darling in every way. And now, should you take it into your head to do me wrong, thinking that I would not know it, you would make a sad mistake.

If you were to let me go ahead without it and then get me caught I would kill every keeper in the place and Dorman with them, and then myself next. I'll tell you, I'm not to be betrayed. I don't say, my dear, that you would try to do me wrong, but you're a woman, and so, as changeable as one, and so I thought I would remind you, knowing that a woman don't look very deep into things Let a woman know you love her and the jig is up Yours,   ED

P S—You did not tell me whether you got the money. What am I to think after waiting this long? You tell me nothing but nonsense I could not stand it My love is too deep for that I would sooner be dead Now, mind after getting through reading this letter make up your mind, then and there, for there is nothing you can say that will keep me another day here and alive Tell me as soon as you can if you are going to stay In case you stay I'll fix it on someone else as near as I can And in case you stay, I will be here to say goodby to you until I see you in March, if you care to see me then And no matter what comes or goes, always remember that your Ed loved you dearly and always will.

Don't say that I am hasty now, for you can't fail to see the predicament we are in this minute — a man on the outside with our secret in his hands Goodby, my own sweet darling I love you now and always will better than anyone in the world Farewell, love from Jack Remember, there will be no changes

There you sit all night with never a word as to whether you had the money, was going to go or do anything, and you were going it to beat the band all afternoon and I could not see a thing you said All you said tonight was a pack of nonsense at such a time as this You told me tonight to write you a letter and you would answer it Well, that means another day

Well, I'll just show you that I'll keep my word I would sooner be in h—— this minute than to stand this

26

anxiety another day, expecting to have to blow my brains out any minute of the day or night I'll tell you, you don't understand it, and you don't seem to care If you weren't in the room tonight and acted funny when my mind was as far from being angry as could be, just in the midst of writing as lovely a letter as any man could ever write to a woman My dear, my heart is almost smothered with love for you as I write it I can see there is a change in your actions and words toward me, and I will not continue one day longer.

THE STORY OF THE ESCAPE.

Graphic Pen Picture of the Desperate Criminals'
Dash for Freedom and Their Attack on the
Guards who Sought to Prevent
Their Flight.

In the dim light of the grim, gray prison which never
dies from one day's dawn until another, the cell tiers
loomed gigantic, like a huge cliff of steel   One above
another, clinging to its sheer face like the fire-escapes
of a factory, but indefinitely prolonged, ran hanging
passages marking the level of the cells, whose grated
doors showed at intervals as oblong patches of deeper
gloom   Behind big windows looked out upon the
lights of the sleeping city, in front towered the preci-
pice of cells, where every dark opening hinted its
tragedy and every shadow that criss-crossed the height
or widened away in the distance to terrifying propor-
tions seemed to conceal a lurking danger

From one of the cells in the third tier a faint light
seemed twice or thrice to glow rather than to shine —
so faint it was that it came to the eyes of the night
keeper, restlessly pacing the stone floor below, not as
something seen but as a subconscious suggestion, di-
verting the mind to thoughts that in such a time and
place bring a shudder.

"This would be just the night for the Biddles to try to break out," he murmured to himself, going noiselessly to the nearest window.

He stood there looking out upon a little paved court, upon a high and gloomy wall beyond, and, further yet, upon a mighty maze of wires that ran along the sky line from the huge telegraph poles set at the curb.

There was something reassuring in the sight "Escape!" he muttered, as he turned away ' Escape with those wires to tell the whole world about it in twenty-nine seconds! This watching must be telling on my nerves!"

But was it an illusion born of long vigils and fancied dangers, or did his strained eyes catch, as he turned away, just the faint suggestion of a flickering answering light in the dark wall opposite him? Even while he wondered — light, indeed, or will-o'-the-wisp of fancy — it was gone, and all was still and somber

Yet not quite still, no jail is ever that Even when in late night before the dawn all its sullen people have yielded to drowsiness, when cautious whispers and rebellious mutterings are no more heard, there is left the rustle of the breathing of unseen men. Sometimes a sigh escapes, sometimes a sob tells of other vigils than those the watchers keep, sometimes there is the noise of restless sleepers turning upon their pallets And through and above it all rises something subtler — as if the walls themselves spoke; as if they caught and held some echo of all the sighs they have heard, of all the deep curses, all the unavailing regrets, passionate threats, repentent vows too long delayed, whispers of hope uttered by lips that quivered, counsels of consolation from brave, broken hearts — as if they caught all this and poured it forth again in a steady, continuous murmur that is of all its components most like a sigh

It is the voice of the jail Those who have imagination can hear it at any time, but it is most insistent, least to be placated, saddest and most bereft of hope in the small hours before dawn

Night Keeper McGarey was one of those who have imagination Often and often he had heard the Voice By the strange fate that rules men's lives it was set down that at night this man was to watch the watchers of desperate prisoners, and by day to write melo-dramas for the New York stage Did the Voice give him hint or whisper of the drama that was soon to unfold itself where he stood? That he of all men is now least able to say as he lies on his bed of suffering

Prosaic enough was the interruption that broke the thread of his thoughts It came from the third tier cell, where once he had fancied that someone was stirring — the faint call of a prisoner for attention

One of the keepers, Reynolds, climbed the stair to the passage on the cliff-face He went along the narrow Way of Sorrows and paused before the cells of the two Biddle brothers, known in the jail as desperate murderers doomed soon to die

" My head aches like the deuce," came a voice from the gloom of one of the cells ' Won't you take my handkerchief and wet it with cold water at the faucet? As cold as you can, that's a good fellow !"

When men's days are numbered and their death watch set, their little requests are honored Reynolds started without a word to do John Biddle's errand.

McGarey had returned to his lonely office, but was still within hail of that great whispering gallery of the night. A far voice now stole down to him, asking for some simple medicine It was close to his hand. Taking it, he started along the lower corridor, climbed the iron stair and reached the cells where the Biddles were confined side by side Reynolds was not in sight.

Between the bars of a cell door McGarey passed the bottle John Biddle took it murmuring thanks Suddenly he grasped McGarey's wrist, and for a moment held it tight

As the clerk strained to release his arm a slight sound caused him to look over his shoulder He saw two sinewy hands grasp, low down, the solid-seeming bars of the next cell, one after another they bent downward and outward They writhed as serpents might in a grasp that holds them harmless, they curved nearly to the floor of the passage And through the opening they had so lately spanned there swiftly pressed a stalwart figure

With a mighty effort McGarey broke loose from the grasp that held him As he turned he looked down the muzzle of a revolver. Behind it a set and resolute eye gleamed from the hardest, strongest face that had ever been seen in all that wall of living graves

Instinctively McGarey backed away to be at longer range The next moment he fell over the railing and was whirling through the air, to fall with a crash upon the stone floor of the corridor He lay there, mangled, motionless, unconscious

Where was the keeper, Peter Soffel, usually so alert, that the tumult did not rouse him?

Dropping John Biddle's handkerchief, Guard Reynolds came leaping up the stairs to the balconied passage Below in the main corridor, another guard, Koslow, ran forward to see what was amiss For

ED. BIDDLE.

an instant the two released convicts grappled in mid-air upon the perilous, narrow passage with Reynolds, then a shot was heard, and he sank to the floor, his hand to his hip

Koslow ran toward the great alarm gong If he could reach it! No! A shot advised him of his peril, the bullet whistled close to his ear.

"I'll blow your head off," said one of the two men in prison garb who leaned over the iron railing, "if you touch that gong" His voice was steady, his arm like steel Koslow stopped and stood while one of the men ran rapidly down the stairs, then the other. Backward, step by step, they cowed him and drove him until he entered the dungeon, and there they locked him in with his own keys They delayed to carry the two wounded men into cells and lay them upon the pallets spread for prisoners Reynolds moaned, for the pain of his shattered hip, but McGarey did not move or make a sound. From his head oozed a drop or two of blood, slowly A more exciting melodrama than he had ever written was acting all about him, the very air was tense with it, but he was unconscious. He saw nothing, heard nothing

Quickly the two men ran to the office, at one end of the long corridor Beyond, they fumbled at a door.

" I must have dropped that d—d key," muttered one

" Break the door!" rejoined his companion, impatiently.

They were still in the part of the building devoted to the jail, but the adjoining living-rooms of the keeper were ahead The door was an ordinary one of deal Together they put their shoulders to it, and it went crashing to the floor. In the room into which they half stumbled, half ran, a woman was waiting

She was tall, with blue eyes widely opened to thoughts of horror, her face round but strongly lined, almost haggard, her teeth glistened white in the dusk of the dimly-lighted library. Though trembling in every limb, she seemed dazed, unable to move. She was caught and held in an irresolution of terror.

And no wonder! For the woman was Kate Soffel, wife of the keeper of the jail The dim lights Keeper McGarey thought he saw had not been fancy Three times a lighted match shaded by the prisoner's hand had signalled from the cell that the attempt would be made that night Once she herself had waved a light from the window of her home to reply that all was ready How many hours had she watched, waited, hoped, despaired, wished that dawn might hasten or might never come!

Now the hour was at hand when she was to leave husband, home, children, friends, good repute, for the love of a man of crime

The younger of the men laid his hand upon her arm as if to wake her "Lively now! The clothes!" he said

"Yes, yes Everything's ready!" she cried, pointing to some garments laid out upon chairs The men hurried away, and in a moment or two returned, dressed in ordinary attire their prison garb left behind forever There was in their attitude that which promised a desperate fight for freedom or for death

The younger was a man of perhaps twenty-six years, but his hard features made him seem older in the light of the library lamp His clean-shaven face was of goodly shape, but a hunted expression glowered in his deep-set, sinister eyes His fine chin was firm and prominent One needed but to look at him to credit all that was said of Edward Biddle's nerve The older man somewhat resembled him, but his eyes were less quick, his chin more softly rounded, his bearing less defiant He seemed equally determined, but perhaps less resourceful One would have looked to John Biddle's brother, not to him, as the leader in their desperate venture.

When the men returned to the library the woman was waiting for them, dressed as if for a walk, and quickly they hurried out into the night, where they were soon lost to sight in the whirling, twirling snow that came drifting down so thickly as to obscure objects a few hundred yards distant

It was the darkest hour, but the happiest either of the three had known for weeks Two had escaped forever from the shadow of the gallows, the third had cast in her lot with them definitely for life or death, and — and anything was better than the haunting suspense, the hesitations, doubts, sudden impulses agonizing conflicts between love and duty she had known so long

Soon they were lost to sight in the city Some known and friendly roof sheltered them — sheltered them well, in all that wild day while the storm raged through Pittsburg's streets, choking them with snow, while edition after edition of the hurrying newspapers told of the escape of Pennsylvania's most famous and most dreaded murderers, no hint of their hiding place was anywhere revealed.

WAS WARDEN CHLOROFORMED?

Slept Heavily while the Biddles were Fighting the
Guards and Making their Escape accom-
panied by His Faithless Wife.

While pistol shots were ringing out in the jail, while
guards were sounding the alarm that told of the Biddles' escape, while all was excitement and turmoil
where was Warden Soffel?

Lying in his bed, sleeping as peacefully as a new-
born babe, all unconscious of what was going on outside, all unmindful that he was needed at his post of
duty. Why was he not awakened? Why did he lie
there slumbering when all this was going on? The
secret was his wife's   She had chloroformed him early
in the evening, as soon as he fell asleep beside her.
Then she had gone out to release her lover, and his
luckless brother   "Where's the Warden?" asked Ed
as she met them outside the prison gates   "He"—
there was a meaning emphasis upon the word — "he
must have been very sound asleep. He never waked
in all that noise"

"Soffel? Oh, he wouldn't wake, not last night!"
The woman spoke easily and naturally, she hardly
seemed to realize that the man of whom she spoke
was her husband, the father of her children. who had

trusted her implicitly, whom she had deceived and

"Did you — did you chloroform him?" whispered John Biddle, after a little break of silence

This time it was the woman who held her peace.

Mrs Soffel never mentioned her husband's name after she was taken It was known that the Warden had already taken steps toward the procuring of a divorce, and he is terribly bitter against the woman who betrayed and ruined him

He now charges that not only did she supply the Biddles with the means of making their escape, but that she chloroformed him in order that there should be no chance of his awaking during the night and interfering with the jailbreak This accounts for the Biddles' daring to go into the Warden's quarters after they had locked the three guards in their cells, although a shorter and easier route out of the jail was open to them.

NEWS OF THE ESCAPE.

The Entire Continent was Shocked and Surprised when it was First made Known that the Warden's Wife was Responsible for it all.

When the news of the escape of the Biddle boys was flashed across the continent on the night of January 30, 1901, it created a sensation from the Atlantic to the Pacific, and the newspaper offices were besieged for particulars. The first detailed dispatch from Pittsburg said:

John and Edward Biddle, two desperadoes with a stirring criminal career, who were in jail here under sentence to be hanged for murder, escaped from the Allegheny County Jail this morning, after seriously injuring two of the guards.

They owe their escape to Mrs. Peter K. Soffel, the wife of the Warden, who had become infatuated with Edward Biddle, a large, handsome man. It was she who furnished the implements of escape and also provided them with weapons. She also went with them.

Warden Soffel made the startling declaration that his wife was involved in the affair. He stated that she is responsible for the furnishing of a revolver and saws to the Biddles, which enabled them to get away.

In her infatuation for the handsome desperado, Edward Biddle, it is said that she has left her husband and her four children, and, is it supposed, is to meet the escaped convicts at a place agreed upon The story of the matter is brief Mrs Soffel was the only person admitted to the jail since last Sunday Yesterday afternoon she visited the condemned men during the Warden's absence.

Last evening she retired at 9 o'clock She told her husband that she was going to visit a sister at McDonald, and that she would retire early, so that she could get an early start Warden Soffel was about the jail until after midnight He retired to his room, which is separate from Mrs Soffel's, shortly before 1 o'clock.

When he awoke this morning he asked for Mrs Soffel, and was informed that she was absent Later, when the details of the escape became known, he telephoned to McDonald, and was informed that she was not there

The Warden then made the following frank confession:

"I believe my wife furnished the weapons to the Biddles and assisted them in making their escape This is an awful thing, but I am only telling the whole truth She was not in bed when I was awakened this morning, and I have not seen her since. She is gone — God only knows where

"I said I would lay everything bare, and I am doing it This is the worst blow of all, but it is true I did not suspect her, and hence was off my guard But she is gone, and the suspicion of assisting in the delivery by furnishing the weapons rests on her"

He broke down and wept when speaking of his wife's actions. "Think of my children," he said. "I would rather have died than come to this. To think that my wife, the last person in the world whom I would suspect, should act so "

Mr Soffel has two girls, 15 and 13 years of age, and two boys, 10 and 7 years old

The ruse of the Biddles was a clever one, and was carried out with great success They sawed out the bars in their cells, John cutting out three in his. Edward, being the larger man, found it necessary to cut out four.

Nothing suspicious was noticed in the actions of the two prisoners, nor was anything wrong discovered when the day guards went off duty yesterday afternoon The murderers evidently sawed the bars during the night, using what appears to have been soap to deaden the noise and to reduce friction

Shortly before 4 o'clock one of the Biddles called to James McGeary, who had charge of the outside gates, and asked for some cramp medicine in a hurry, saying his brother was dangerously sick McGeary hastened to the cell with the medicine, when John Biddle sprang through the opening in the cell and, seizing the guard around the waist, hurled him over the railing to the stone floor beneath, a distance of sixteen feet

Edward Biddle joined his brother immediately, and both, with drawn revolvers, hurried to the first floor, where they met Guard Reynolds and shot him

There were but three men on duty, and the third was on one of the upper ranges. He was ordered down at the point of revolvers, and the three guards were put in the dungeon.

The keys were taken from Keeper McGeary, and the two prisoners had a clear field. The only persons who witnessed the escape were prisoners, who could not interfere or give an alarm. The Biddles went to the wardrobe where the guards keep their clothing, and each put on a new suit. They then unlocked the outside gates and passed out into Ross street

The escape was not discovered until the daylight guards came on duty at 6 o'clock. They were informed by prisoners where the night guards had been put, and the latter were soon released from the dungeon and sent to the Homeopathic Hospital

The two guards injured will probably recover. The bullet wound sustained by Reynolds is not regarded as dangerous. The physicians have been unable to ascertain as yet the full extent of McGeary's wounds. His head is badly contused, but there are no signs that his skull was fractured by his sixteen-foot fall.

The Prison Board began an investigation this afternoon, and announced upon adjournment tonight that Warden Soffel, at his own request, had been relieved from duty, pending the result of the investigation. Deputy Warden Marshal was placed in charge temporarily. Nothing else was given out. James Francis Burke and J. D. Watson, the attorneys who defended the Biddles at the trial, and the former of whom was instrumental in securing their respite, have announced that their connection with the case is ended, and Attorney Burke has telegraphed the Governor that the application for a hearing before the Pardon Board is withdrawn.

The friends of Mrs. Soffel believe that she could not have been in her right mind when she aided in the escape of the Biddles. For some years she has been an invalid, and about a year ago she was sent to a sanitarium. She came back very much improved, but the long and painful illness is believed to have weakened her mind.

Her husband devoted time and money for the relief of the suffering of his wife, but it is said that she never has fully recovered her health, and at times was melancholy.

WAS MRS. SOFFEL'S FATHER AN ACCOMPLICE?

Her Husband had him Dismissed from the Prison Service, where he was Guard, and Charges him with Fostering the Love of his Truant Wife for the Convicts.

Warden Peter Soffel, soon after the escape and the flight of his faithless wife, charged C H Dietrich, his father-in-law, with being an accomplice of his wife in the escape of the Biddles, and on this charge Dietrich, who was a prison guard, was summarily dismissed from the service

He knew, it is said, of his daughter's love for Biddle, and as deputy warden, it is alleged, he allowed the thing to go on with a slight remonstrance

Warden Soffel peremptorily demanded the dismissal of his father-in-law from the jail force, and now declares that he was a Biddle accomplice The Warden threatened to kill him on sight

Dietrich told some of the neighbors, however, and it was corroborated by the jail officers, that Mrs Soffel had her attention attracted to Edward Biddle shortly after he was convicted of the murder of Grocer Kahney.

The murdered man had been a neighbor of the Dietrichs and the Soffels. The cells in Murderers' Row occupied by the Biddles could be seen from the room occupied by Mrs. Soffel in the jail, and Edward used to sit in his cell and cast longing glances at the woman His appearance at first was that of a dejected mortal

Gradually it lit with pleasure every time she appeared at the window Emboldened by pitying glances, Edward, like a caged tiger, centered his efforts on Mrs Soffel, until she finally succumbed.

The guards were aware of the flirtation, and it is said Mr Dietrich called his daughter's attention to the impropriety of her conduct

He says she did not answer him, and when he accused her of being in love with Edward Biddle, after she had begun visiting him at his cell, she turned on her heel and walked away The guards used to discuss the jail flirtation, but everyone kept it secret from Warden Soffel.

But Mrs Soffel was not the only one who was brought under the spell of the condemned men.

The guards, including Mr Dietrich, all sympathized with the Biddles Edward was frank with them He told them of the many crimes he had committed, but persistently said he and his brother did not commit the Kahney crime, and that he did not kill Fitzgerald; that it was Inspector Bob Gray's shot that ended Fitzgerald's life

Mr Dietrich said " I discovered her infatuation for the Biddles several months ago I repeatedly warned her to cease her flirtations from the Warden's residence I asked whether she was infatuated with Edward Biddle, but she never made reply.

" About two weeks ago Ed Biddle asked me to take some poetry he had written to my daughter, and I agreed. I brought it home, and on Monday or Tues-

44

day, when Kate was here, I gave it to her. I did not look at it, and when my daughter asked me to take some books back to Biddle I refused, and told her that if she wanted to do anything of that kind she must get her husband to do it, I would not

"The actions of my daughter caused suspicion in the jail and considerable talk. But I never thought she would do what she did. When I went to work Wednesday evening at 6 o'clock Edward Biddle asked me for matches. Some time later I heard Edward Biddle ask one of the guards for a match. I thought this suspicious, as I had given him a whole box.

"About 11 o'clock I called the attention of one of the guards to the reflection of a light on the window of my daughter's room in the Warden's house. I assumed that it was from a match in the cell of Ed Biddle. It was not long before there was another light, casting the same reflection. I called the attention of one of the guards to this, and told him that it looked very suspicious. I figured out that Edward wanted the matches to signal to my daughter. I informed no one about it, as the guards with me also saw it.

"It was about this time that McGarey remarked that he had a suspicion that the Biddles would attempt to escape.

"I did not inform Warden Soffel about it. He knew of the visits of my daughter to the cell. I had a suspicion that an attempt to escape would be made, because the Biddles were awake. Jack Biddle was sitting up in the cell, but Ed had covered himself up. I had some fresh doughnuts that I had taken from home, and I offered one to Ed. He accepted, and seemed thoroughly awake. I did not give one to Jack."

45

MRS. SOFFEL'S DEVOTION.

She was the Mysterious Veiled Woman who Pleaded
with Governor Stone for the Lives of the
Biddles, and finding further Sup-
plication Useless, Released
them Herself.

A week prior to the sensational escape and its tragic
ending a tall, stately woman, closely veiled, visited Governor Stone at Harrisburg, and pleaded with him for
the life of the Biddle boys She was hysterical, and
fell on her knees to the Governor and begged him to
spare their lives She told him she knew they were
innocent, and were so young and handsome it was
awful that they must die on the gallows She wept
copiously as she pleaded, and the Governor was duly
impressed He told her he could not grant them a
pardon, but he would grant them a respite in order
that the Board of Pardons could review the case and
recommend a commutation of sentence to life imprisonment, if they thought such commutation should be
made This seemed to lighten her spirts greatly, and
she promised to go before the Board of Pardons and
renew her supplications that their lives be spared She
did not tell the Governor who she was, and begged
him not to tell anyone she had been to see him or the

nature of her errand She displayed a well-filled purse, and said she would spend any amount to save the two young men from their ignominious fate, or go to any extreme to secure for them life imprisonment instead of the death penalty After she left the executive he wrote out the respites and forwarded them to Warden Soffel. Little did he dream the woman at whose pleadings he was granting them was the Warder's wife! Until the awful disclosures later, he never even suspected that such was the case, and it was a great surprise when he did learn it Since her capture Mrs Soffel has admitted it was she who pleaded with Governor Stone for the life of the man she had so foolishly learned to love, and that of his erring brother She said she deceived her husband, and when she went to Harrisburg told him she was going to visit her mother, who lives there He had not the slightest suspicion she was more than passingly interested in the condemned men, and made no objection to her trip to the State Capital.

JACK BIDDLE.

STRANGE POWER OF ED. RIDDLE.

Mysterious Influence he Exerted over Women whom
he Seemed to Attract and Hypnotize by
some Mysterious Power.

The influence Ed Biddle exercised over women was
most remarkable It seems he had but to fix his eye
on a woman and she was fated to do his bidding, whatever it might be The influence with which he swayed
the frail wife of the prison warden has electrified the
entire country and mystified those students of human
nature whose long experience has shown them many
cases of the power of one mind over another When
wealthy and fashionable women of the city sent him
flowers and fruit and showed in a variety of other
ways that their interest in him was more than that
which usually falls to the lot of a criminal, these students of human nature stood by and wondered

There seemed to be some occult power born and
dominant in this man It manifested itself in ways
various and detrimental, to the positive knowledge of
the Pittsburg authorities. His strange fascination over
the Zeebers woman, his willing tool and partner in
his crimes, is well known.

In Butler this same magic influence was felt Many
were the expressions of sympathy heard Many were the

49

words of condemnation hurled at the heads of the detectives for resorting to methods which are here considered cruel and barbarous

One of the physicians was bending over the murderer in his cell. He was tenderly stroking his hair and asking him, in a voice as tender as a woman's, if he could do anything for him. Only a glance of vacancy was the reward of his solicitude, and he turned from the cot of the dying man with a sigh laden with sorrow and sympathy

"These men have told us several stories since they were admitted here," he said, "and I have noticed that what they have said agreed in the main. I am inclined to believe what they say"

"And so was Mrs Soffel," ventured the reporter; and that confidence led her to the Butler Hospital." But the physician only shook his head. The fatal fascination made itself felt

It has been established that no less than twenty-five women of Pittsburg were working at one time to save them from the gallows

Mrs Soffel was the master spirit of this coterie. Her coworkers were the wives of well-known business men, and two of them were Sisters of Mercy from the Webster Avenue Convent. The Rev Father Sweeney lent his encouragement

On Christmas Day the Biddles received Holy Communion, after the rites of the Catholic Church. They devoutly expressed their contrition for their past misdeeds, and declared their change of heart

Two Sisters from the Webster Avenue Convent visited them in jail soon after this. Soffel met them and talked with them.

Soon the scheme to save them from the gibbet took form. The nuns solicited money. Mrs. Sofiel enlisted the aid of other women. Members of the St. Vincent de Paul Society at the Cathedral assisted, though in no way pledging the sanction of the organization itself.

Letters were written to more than a score of the most prominent business men in the city. The persecution of the Biddles was set forth. Their innocence of many of the crimes laid at their door was asserted. Virtues many and admirable were attributed to them.

Not one of these letters was ever answered. Not a cent was added to the fund through them.

Here comes the strangest part of the story.

The leaders of the movement turned from the men to their wives. The influence of the Biddles appeared. Every woman answered the appeal.

The part played in the raising of funds by the Sisters of Mercy has been misrepresented.

Sister Inez, Mother-Superior of the Webster Avenue Convent, issued the following statement: "It is true that I took an interest in the Biddle brothers, believing that they were not as bad as they were painted. Money was solicited among friends. All of it was turned over to their attorneys. None of it went to the Biddles or to Mrs. Sofiel."

This statement is to be given official circulation in church circles. There were women that not only gave money to the fund for saving the men, but had masses said for them. This was established recently.

It is almost without parallel in the city's history. A member of the Cathedral Society has said:

"From the moment the Biddles stated to Father Sweeney that they were innocent of the Kahney and

Fitzgerald murders, and showed signs of having under-gone a change of heart, they found their way into the sympathies of hundreds

"Even the memory of the robberies to which they confessed was forgotten I myself solicited money for them But the strangest part of the whole story is the writing of the letters

"Letters were sent to nearly every prominent busi-ness man in the city, irrespective of religious belief. It was not a matter of religion, but of what we thought justice Not one answer to all these letters was re-ceived

"I saw that sensible men concluded the law should take its course, and withdrew.

"The women turned the tables, and succeeded par-tially

Instead of writing to the heads of families of prom-inence, they appealed to their wives."

Soffel-Biddle Alphabetical Code.

A cipher code found in Mrs Soffel's room showed that by pointing to her forehead Ed Biddle, in his cell opposite her window, knew she was spelling the letter A Pointing to her eyes meant B and C, to the tip of her nose D, and so on, her chin, ears, mouth, shoulders, breasts and elbows having special significance Clasping her hands meant a period at the end of a sentence Th s code was used for weeks by the conspiring couple

THE FLIGHT FOR LIFE.

Terrible Sufferings of the Fugitives in the Blinding Snow and Freezing Cold of a Northern Winter.

Often in the keen cold of a Northern winter morning dawns on the stiff, stark body of some poor unfortunate traveler or outcast who has struggled to the utmost limit of human endurance and has fallen to rise no more. Often over the vast white wastes soar the slow-flying buzzards, looking for just such prey. When the fugitives started next morning from the house that had sheltered them that one eventful night they well knew the desperate chances they were taking and that the chances were terribly against them. There was death ahead of them, and death behind them. Death lurked on every side. How much better death peacefully amid that pure white snow than a terrible end on the grim, black gallows. With the snow cruelly beating in their faces, they plodded along for hours. In vain they begged the woman to go back, and told her she would perish. "I have given all for you. Do you mean to desert me?" she asked pleadingly of her lover, Ld. "No, you've stuck to us, and we'll stick to you," he replied with brigandish chivalry. And on they floundered together. The cold was intense, the wind bitter, and the snow wearying and tiresome. Miles after miles they tramped along in silence, every moment expecting their pursuers to show up behind them on their trail With hands on the butts of their revolvers they staggered onward, resolved, if it came to the worst, to make the fight of their lives for their lives, or death not so shameful as that to which they were doomed by the relentless law Then, grown desperate and fearing that they might fall down and die upon the road, they broke into a country school-house It furnished shelter from the wind, but bleak comfort They dared not light a fire, though perhaps they might have done so safely There was but one line of railroad in the great stretch of farming country between Economy, in the west, and Culmerville, in the east, that lay before them In that wide zone of quiet homes few people would have been stirring in the early morning hours of bitter night, and any that there might have been would have thought twice before interfering with what we must suppose the safe shelter of a harmless tramp

But these were no tramps, to wander care-free and at will, something sterner than the poormaster was through all the bleak, dreary hours that seemed to their impatience endless, they paced up and down the aisles of the little schoolroom with its whittled desks, its scrawled blackboard, its countless reminders of rosy childhood They read in the copybooks in cramped characters traced by baby fingers the little writings of the pupils who had been taught the little writings of the pupils who had been taught there before the snow fell so fast and furious the children could not get to school and the little schoolhouse had been closed up. The luckless woman thought of her own little ones at home, and she wept in her anguish and remorse. But it was too late for tears and regrets now The road to safety, aye to life its very self, lay ahead Out into the cruel cold the trio started again, blindly almost, trudging along away from Pittsburg and the grim prison which they had left behind, they hoped, forever The snow still pelted mercilessly down, and their tired and aching limbs were growing stiffer with the cold every minute Suddenly Ed Biddle said " If I'm not mistaken, there's the railroad ahead Now, mind, we're looking for an old maid aunt — she lives away beyond, somewhere — up Peterville way "

It was the railroad track — the one that wanders lonesomely up from Sharpsburg to Callery Junction across the great island of quiet between the humming webs of rails to East and West And the name of the place where they crossed it was Talley Cavey — Dickens in his wildest fancy never invented such a name; but there it stood for years upon the map of grave old Pennsylvania, waiting for a great tragedy, a great struggle and a great sacrifice to bring it for a day to passing notice of the whole land

On, on they tramped across the desolate country, over the hard, white surface Now the day gradually wore away and the gray of twilight began to lower with the coming of night Their condition was by this time growing unbearable They were starving and freezing, and feared they could never outlive the night if they did not soon get indoors or under shelter. About despairing, they struggled on with endurance born of desperation Suddenly Ed, the keen - eyed watcher of the party, raised his head with an exclamation and pointed toward a low-lying shed away to the right " Wait here by this tree," he said, and a moment later he was bounding off toward the little shanty In fear and trembling they awaited his return. They did

56

not have to wait long. In less time than it takes to tell it they heard a jingle of sleighbells, and Ed came dashing back to them in a sleigh drawn by a big gray horse 'Jump in, quick!" he yelled; "for the man I borrowed this team from might want it back" In they jumped, and off they went as hard as the old horse could travel, while the owner of the team sat beside his fireside away behind, all in ignorance that his team had been stolen That night's ride was the wildest men or women ever endured With only scant blankets and a few old bags Ed had tossed into the sleigh, they made the trembling woman crouch down in the bottom of the sleigh, to better shield her from the bitter cold All through the night they drove on, and for hours they drove steadily ahead, and Nature began to assert herself They must have food and rest They could not endure the cold longer, with starving stomachs and aching limbs.

"This is better," said Edward Biddle cheerfully, as the white landscape slipped by, field by field, tiny house and big barn after big barn and tiny house, all half-buried in snow "We'll have to stop for breakfast somewhere, or die of cold; but there's no help for that Must take some chances, of course When the farmer who owns this big bag of bones misses it there'll be a commotion anyhow"

"Oh, I dread to stop," cried Kate Soffel "I dread to stop! If I could be sure that I wasn't delaying you, keeping you back—"

"Never fear!" Edward Biddle almost gayly responded "It's all right now we're out in the open Let anyone try to stop me now! If I was to die next minute I wouldn't leave you, after all you've done for us!"

"I couldn't bear to see you die so — and innocent—"

"Poor woman! Never mind, we must get across the railroad somewhere, then we'll stop at any farmhouse Wherever it may be there'll be a woman in it, and she'll be kind and glad to see us. If the world were all like the women in it men wouldn't drive men as they do, wouldn't hound 'em to crime and hound 'em after it, and kick 'em when they're down!"

"Ah, the women!" said the woman who listened; and there was a sudden ring of jealousy in her tone. "Ed! Ed! After all this — after — oh, don't you ever leave me, Ed! I couldn't bear it! There's no place for me in the world except the place we make for each other"   ❧

"I shan't forget that But you mustn't want me to forget all the good women who've pitied and helped me No man ever crooked his finger to save my neck It was a woman who got the Governor to reprieve us It was a girl who left the book of peoms — you remember the little verses I wrote for her on the flyleaf — 'Just a little violet from across the way' —oh, well, I'll never see any of 'em again. Just let me tell you—"

It was Edward who drove, from his seat upon the right side of the cutter. He flicked the snow with his whip as he mused for a moment over grim recollections.

Once that bitter evening the men wavered in their fight with Nature Used to the cold air of the jail, they shivered in the cold And the windows of a little road house blinked invitingly at them.

"Let's go in and get warm for a few minutes," said John Biddle, stopping in front of the swinging sign.

"Not me," Kate Soffel replied, with instant decision. "Two men and a woman? They're looking for just such a party No — but you go in, you two I'll wait"

The men hesitated, they faltered, they accepted the offer and went in A little further along the road Mrs Soffel waited for them, while they drank the stuff that keeps away chill for a time, and later surrenders at discretion

Under the warming influence of their stop the men were for a time more cheerful

"How queer things turn out,' mused Edward Biddle, as they resumed their journey and he glanced up at the stars he had seen of late only from the barred cell of the doomed "Seems hardly possible — and three months ago I did not know you!"

"Three months — and all that has happened!" the woman replied with a little shudder "Oh, Ed! Ed! A hundred times it has seemed as if I couldn't keep the secret any longer! When I bought the saws and the revolvers in McKeesport — when I had to carry my secret about, day after day — oh, my heart was in my mouth! I'm happier now! If we could only—"

'Lake Erie's ahead," said John Biddle, cheerfully "Only a hundred miles away We could foot it in four days — less than that if it wasn't for the cold. If we could somehow get into Canada—"

"Never mind Canada!" cried the woman, passionately "It's good to be here where we can talk — and nobody but the stars to listen! I don't believe you know, either of you, what I've suffered since that day last November when I saw you first, Ed Biddle! I did so want to help you! I couldn't bear to have them take you away and kill you, but it was hard to know what I ought to do   When my own father charged me with loving you I couldn't deny it   I could only turn away so that my face shouldn't tell everything

There was homely cheer in the dining-room of the little country hotel at Cooperstown   A generous meal graced the table with its spotless cloth, the hostlers in the Liberty Barns were giving the jaded horse as kindly a welcome, and the landlord and his wife attended to the wants of their guests   Perhaps, too, they were more than willing to linger and chat awhile with the chance passers from the world outside who were likely to be their only customers that bitter morning.

It was a scene for the painter of homely, homelike scenes.   The guests, their fierce hunger sated, lingered at the table, willing to delay a little longer their battle with the cold   The landlord sat with them, happily steaming in the heat, his coat thrown off, his rugged face shining with good nature and native kindness, while his better-half bustled about, hastening to rejoin and lingering to leave the cozy half-circle as her duties called   A girl of a dozen years hung about her father's knee, shyly noticing everything.

"We'd never have started if we'd dreamed the weather would turn so harsh," Edward Biddle was explaining   "It doesn't look far on the map, but the roads are awful and the cold worse   I don't think they gave us a good horse, either"

The landlord exploded in sudden mirth   "Good horse!" he roared   "That's the trouble.   Can't see whether the horse is good or not, 'cause ye can't see him at all   Ye see right through him!   Now, ef they'd fatten up that horse a year or so, then ye might get so's to look at him and see if he was any good   And I wouldn't wonder if 'twas, at that; only he's been

hungry and tired too long. Say, if ye do freeze to
death anywheres along th' road, that liveryman ought
to be jailed for hiring you such a bunch of bones and
charging you for hoss hire" Then he laughed heartily
at what he considered his good joke After refreshing
themselves and their jaded steed, they would well have
liked to have had a sleep in the nice, large, comfortable
rooms of the old hotel, but there was not time to be
lost They must be off Even then their pursuers
might be closing in on them and getting ready to complete the final act in the drama which was so soon
to become a tragedy

And so, with many a hospitable message shouted
after them, and much advice as to the road, and hearty
wishes for their safe arrival, the three set out again
upon their weary fight with snow and cold and with
the pack that bayed upon their trail

It could not have added to their comfort in the
breakfast they had eaten, the fire they had sat beside,
the good people that had cheered them, if they could
hav known how soon after their departure the story
of the broken jail and the three fugitives was to be
discussed at the fireside they had quitted, that the
little girl who had exclaimed at the "city lady's" rings
was to be the first to identify her as the missing jailer's
wife from her face pictured in the newspapers and
set the trailers at their heels

On and on and on! Endless wastes of snow, weary
miles of road, a horse that lagged more and more
with every step. Indeed, it was not so bad a horse as
the joking farmer claimed — a little gaunt, but sound
and willing — but it was overdriven now, and tired
And Butler was just ahead Butler with many fast
trains each day, with newspapers by the thousands in

61

times of excitement like this — Butler, with its five lmes of meeting tracks, its county buildings, and, of course, its Sheriff's deputies The landlord had given them explicit directions for finding Butler, which they now used to avoid it, carefully seeking out crossroads that took them a mile to the west, within sight of its spires, almost within sound of its hum and bustle

And now once more their way was clear before them — another great block of open country lay ahead where ran no gleaming rails for twenty miles to east and west and more than twenty miles to the north But in these days the telephone threads every wilderness. And there would be rewards offered, big enough to tempt the hunters of men Henceforth they should go warily, should slink from the sight of human beings, however friendly they might seem, they must trust only themselves — must in some way — and quickly, quickly, throw the hounds of the law off the trail

But the day grew colder rather than warmer There was in their veins the stored chill of the night, of weary walking in the snow, of the drive through the dawn — a little, perhaps, the chill of waning courage, of resolution once more needing the sustenance of food and warmth and shelter They stopped for a late luncheon at a tiny hotel in Chestnut Mount While they ate a big two-horse sleigh drove rapidly past the door There were half a dozen men upon the seats, and the horses sped merrily along under the hardly needed urging of a skilful driver Hidden beneath the robes was a whole armament of weapons

For the moment the hounds had overshot the trail, and the Biddle party were safe.

THE BEGINNING OF THE END.

The Chase Draws to a Close as the Pursuers get Hot on the Trail of their Desperate Prey and the Final Tragic Finale is Close in Sight.

Perhaps they would plunge blindly on, and they would yet escape, but they must up and away, lest they should return. Quickly leaving their half-finished meal, they hitched up the poor, tired old horse and, bundling into the sleigh, started off again. The landlord scented something queer in their sudden departure and their leaving their meals unfinished He was soon to know why It was to the northwest that they turned when at last they were under way It was fate

The tired horse was hardly to be goaded past a walk, but cruelly they plied him with the whip By degrees he was warmed into clumsy action, and swung at a slow trot through as pretty a bit of rural country as Western Pennsylvania can furnish Everywhere about them was snow, scintillant in the sun, the snow that would reveal every trace of their feet should they abandon their horse and take to the fields There was —there seemed to be—but one course open They pushed ahead

It is hardly four miles from Mount Chestnut to Prospect, and they were to travel only half the way;

but even this little distance seemed to their sleepless impatience almost unending   At last, as they crept up a long slope to its rounded summit, the ears of a pair of horses rapidly driven showed above the virgin white line of its crest

A moment more and they knew that Fate was face to face with them.

THE FIGHT TO THE DEATH.

Desperate Duel in the Snow Between the Fugitives
and their Pursuers which had a most
Tragic Ending.

Flight was no impossible, evasion was no longer a
tenable hope! The pursuers had doubled on their trail
and were coming back after them. Well they knew
what that meant. It meant all was over, that the end
was in sight, and that the battle to the death was near
at hand. Every step they had taken in their long,
stubborn fight with the cold now lay revealed to their
pursuers. The roadhouse where they had paused for
a few minutes on the evening of their escape, the house
where they had breakfasted, the hamlets they had
passed had spread the news to them. The little hotel
at Mount Chestnut had indeed sheltered them for a
moment while the chase swept past, but the telephone
had woven a net about them, and the way to Canada
was blocked. It was 5 o'clock of a cloudless but
piercingly cold winter day. The sun had just set;
the North Star that had led them was not yet visible.
There was more than light enough to fight by.

And there were fighting men before them, armed
to the teeth with deadly Colts and Winchesters — five
in one sleigh, three in another. They were closing

65

in around the flying fugitives who were trying to make their poor old jaded horse move faster than he was able It was useless for further effort They might as well have laid down their arms and surrendered, but that would have meant the awful death by the noose It was better for them to die like men fighting, than like dogs with ropes around their necks They made the last stand and, drawing their revolvers, they made ready for the fray The weeping, trembling, hysterical woman lay flat on the bottom of the sleigh. "Don't cry," said Ed softly, "it'll soon be over now"

"Crack!"

A puff of white smoke, and a rifle ball shrieked past their heads

"Crack!"

Ed's big Colt revolver answered the shots with lightning rapidity

Death was in the air menaced from the stern faces; sounded in their muttered cautions Save death there was no possible outcome From the right side of the little cutter Ed Biddle leaped out, to the left of his brother The younger man raised a shotgun stolen from the hotel in Mount Chestnut It was a poor weapon, and what its charge might be he did not know; but he fired as best he could with numb fingers at the nearest man The harmless bird shot scattered wide of the mark The next moment there was a rattle of small arms

It was all over in a few frenzied moments — what chance was there? The runaways, their one shot from the gun expended, had only the revolvers which they had been able to conceal in their cells Upon them were levelled revolvers of superior caliber, and long rifles held by steady arms not numbed with cold, not tremulous from vigils, hardships and lack of sleep

Twice shot, Ed Biddle deliberately placed his revolver over his own heart and fired Bleeding from a dozen wounds, John Biddle sought quick death by firing twice, his pistol pressed against his own mouth Not one of those that both had fired at the officers had found its billet To right and left the desperate men reeled and fell

A cruel bullet found its way into the breast of Mrs Soffel Some say Ed Biddle fired it to end her misery, some say she shot herself But it is more than likely it was from the revolver of one of the officers who stood in the road pouring a shower of lead at the helpless and poor wounded two With a shriek she cowered down, crying " Oh, my God ! Ed, I'm shot !" " Bang, bang !" went the pistols of the pursuers as they closed in about their prey, who lay weltering in their life blood

It was an awful scene The red in the west was paling, but daylight lingered, caught and held and reflected by the mantle of snow that muffled every object, turning the fences to fantastic shapes in billowing white, clothing the fields deeply for their winter sleep From one or two distant chimneys curled and drifted the smoke of wood fires replenished for the cooking of supper And on the snow, just where it was most trampled by men and horses in this little war of outlawry, were scattered stains of blood, and two men lay, ghastly pale, but unsubdued, prone on its soft white bed. One still struggled to aim a final shot, when a fighting man from the line, closing in upon them, fired at close range and battered down the last resistance with his clubbed rifle.

And the woman — the guilty, suffering, sacrificing, foolishly fond woman — to her in these fleeting moments of the fight no one had paid attention No one had fired at her or perhaps thought of her Now she rose and stood swaying in the frail cutter as the frightened horse gathered its strength for a bolt, then, as the maddened animal dashed at the fence, it is said, she thrust her hand within her jacket and fired in the hope of piercing her own heart She fell in a huddle in the bottom of the cutter

The horse plunged more wildly, one of the detectives shot him to stop him from running away Poor beast! It had seen many strange experiences in the thirteen or fourteen hours since it left its stable, and now to be shot in a war never of its own choosing! It's the way of the world!

Another of the detectives raised gently the fallen woman and placed his hand over her heart It beat strongly Her life had been as resolute as her sin, her waist was torn by the bullet But a corset steel had turned aside the bullet, and those who gathered about her with awkward sympathy knew that she would live Her punishment was to be the worst of all — the worst that human imagination can conceive The woman pays!

The sudden clamor had sunk into silence One could almost doubt the gunshots, the passionate defiance, the relentless onset, the sound of blows It was with hushed voices and gentle hands that the men lifted the three who together had suffered and struggled and fought, and set out upon the six-mile drive back to Butler Crossroads had not availed them in avoiding it as, in the wild life they had led, crossroads of straying from the right forbidden bypaths and stolen excursions, had brought them at the last to this end, where the only good that could be said of them was that they had been brave, the only hope that might be felt for them was that they might not live.

MRS. SOFFEL'S STORY.

Her Version of the Whole Affair from Her Own Lips in the Jail Hospital.

When grim and awful Fate chose Mrs. Kate Soffel to undergo experiences that would have killed ninety-nine women out of a hundred, when love and weakness led this woman to commit a most heroic, as well as a most revolting crime, one — just one — sweet drop was added to her bitter cup. Chance sent her to the Butler Hospital.

From the window of the room where Mrs Soffel lay one looked out from an eminence over the dark pine laden with snow, and the peaceful little sloping town, and away from the height upon which this hospital is located. A quieter, more beautiful spot Nature never created for the healing of a bruised and tired spirit Mrs. Soffel took the hand of the nurse between hers.

" If I had been sinless," she said, stroking the strong, steady little hand she held in her blue, shaky ones, " if I had hundreds of friends, if I had been really good to you, you couldn't have done more for me in this blessed, peaceful place. Oh, if they only won't take me away.

" I can't bear the idea of their taking me from here. You didn't look at me as if you liked me," she went on, her breast, with its dressing packed over the bullet wounds over her heart, heaving with short, agitated gasps ' I knew you didn't pity me when you saw me the first day down at the jail, but now you like me a little, don't you? Oh, if you can, keep me here in this quiet place Let me get well, oh, let me get strong before I go back to face what I must."

Imagine what this woman went through before she came to this haven, this little hospital on a hill, too human to be institutional, too little patronized to have a criminal ward, too isolated to take misery and vice for granted and philosophically to ignore or endure them. Imagine that terrible ride out in the snow-covered hills with that behind her which sent her recklessly forward, even to death.

" For forty-eight hours I hadn't eaten I couldn't have eaten. My heart was in my throat All my life, and all my blood, seemed choked and dammed up right at my throat It wasn't the cold so much, though I couldn't get warm for hours after they put me in bed And it wasn't the terror nor the anxiety, but that awful feeling that my throat was choking and must burst before I could breathe."

She is still hysterical, this woman, whose amazing daring, whose thorough and complete sacrifice has something that is heroic, as well as everything that is shameful, in them.

As she lay flat upon her back, her head level almost with her body, not able to lift herself an inch from the bed, her breath came in pitiful, short gasps and hysterical catches told of the suffering she endured

72

For Kate Soffel will live, and she knows it now, and knows, too, what life has in store for her This is the reason for her misery Her wound is the least that ails her The bullet which struck her in the left breast, and which, it is alleged, Ed Biddle fired with the intention of ending her life with theirs, has been extracted, and the wound in fast healing Dr. McAlpin, who attended her at the hospital, said " She is a very strong woman "

" Yes, I am " Mrs Soffel's heavy lids lifted. " Too strong, too strong A weaker woman would have got pneumonia

" A weaker woman would have died from cold and shock. But I, I must live Oh, God, if 1 could die Oh, God, if I could die Just one inch to the right Just one little inch, and I wouldn't have to stay to bear it all alone."

There is no doubt that this woman is sincere in her wish Life holds so much that is fearful to her that death has no terrors in comparison.

" I felt the bullet go in," she said, in one of the intervals when she waked from her moaning sleep. She moaned, not from pain, but because of mental anguish that is almost unendurable

" And I hoped it would kill me And all the time I was conscious I heard that brute, McGovern, come sneering around the operating table when I lay there ' D'ye know me?' he shouted ' I'm McGovern, the detective '

"Oh, I knew him. He was the McGovern that shot that poor boy Ed Biddle when he was handcuffed, lying on the ground, with the blood streaming from him. He was the McGovern that hit him over the head in the sleigh. God knows what else he did I heard the men who were bringing me into town say 'There they go, they're not through with their fireworks yet.' Fireworks! Oh, God, I can see it yet I will never, never get it out of my sight Those fifteen men opening fire upon two boys and a woman What's that? Ed Biddle fire first? Not much They gave him no chance It was an army of men against those two. All the shots those poor boys fired were fired at themselves

Mrs Soffel's voice showed the weakness of extreme exhaustion, and she rarely spoke at length But her voice grew strong with horror and with scorn when she spoke of one of the attacking party, whose brutality she dwelt upon, though two of its members she remembered with gratitude.

"I had not intended going with the Biddle boys on the night of the escape, but Ed's entreaties won me over "

She told of how she remained in the library on Thursday morning, awaiting the signal for the outbreak It was her intention to let the boys go, and she would meet them later While sitting in the library she was almost paralyzed when the two brothers came crashing through the door. In their excitement they had lost the key to this door, and had to break it down

"Ed asked me to come with them 'Come with us,' he said to me I resisted and told them to go They told me they had not an instant to lose and if the officers were to get away I would be discovered.

"I tried to persuade them to go Then I felt myself giving way to Ed's persuasions, and yielded

"We all dashed out on Ross street We then passed along the Courthouse to the alley Ed and Jack went out Grant street, and, crossing the river, we met in

Allegheny at their friend's house. Well, we could not remain there. The hours in the schoolhouse were perishing cold. The exposure affected me greatly.

"Now, I want to say the statements that I was intoxicated are untrue Ed and Jack bought a half-pint of whiskey, and I drank some of it It seemed to stimulate me Now, that was the only time I drank anything on the trip

"Ed and Jack took several drinks, and I told them to go sparingly on it, as they would not be able to get any more without enhancing detection We secured a sleigh and drove through the country all night. The night was bitter cold There was no robe in the sleigh, and I suffered terribly When daylight came I was nearly perished by the cold

"Well, the next day brought us to the terrible scene We drove past Butler, and knew that we had been suspected.

"Then we soon reached Mount Chestnut, and, getting something to eat, started out again I was feeling ill, and was frightened The boys learned that the detectives were after us, and they consulted about defending themselves Ed said to Jack, 'It is a life for a life, let's shoot them down'"

"The boys drove on They were bewildered about the whereabouts of the detectives They thought the Pittsburg detectives were behind them.

"When they saw them appear Ed told Jack to get ready He recognized Detective Roach

"Detective McGovern got out of the sleigh, and was followed by the other two I saw Detective McGovern fire The two shots were returned by Ed and Jack. Then there was a fusilale of bullets. I saw Ed and Jack fall out of the sleigh

" I was shot. The horse took fright and ran away.

" Detective McGovern said . Kill all the d—— ras-
cals, and pointed his gun at me.

" Detective Swinehart called to him to have mercy
on me, that I was only a woman, and not to shoot me

, " The horse turned into the field and made a circle
into the road again

" I didn't fall out of the sleigh   I jumped out.   I
now remember setting my feet on the step, and then;
in jumping, I fell   That was all I remember.   Detective Swinehart ran to me, and, calling to me, he
asked if I was hurt, and I said I was shot   He raised
me up and held my head on his knees   Then I felt
myself fainting, and the next thing I knew I was
in the sleigh.   We arrived at the jail, and the rest is all
known.

" It is my gratitude to Detective Swinehart for his
treatment of me and saving me from being shot down.
The detectives were justified in shooting at the boys,
for they intended to kill them

: " We were forced to leave the jail before our ar-
rangements were complete   I learned on Wednesday
that the bars on the doors of the cells on that range
were to be inspected on Thursday.   I knew the sawed
bars on Ed and Jack s cell would be discovered.   I
gained admittance to the jail, and conveyed this information to the boys   We then agreed to go that
night   I did not intend to go with them   They were
to make their flight alone   I intended to go to the
country for a few days, and then meet them

Mrs Soffel is taking steps to defend herself, and
has written to a prominent Pittsburg attorney to engage his services.   Her father is said to be quite well-

to-do, and as her parents **are** relenting she hopes to receive aid from them

The Prison Board is satisfied Mrs Soffel had assistance within the prison walls, and before the Biddle incident is finally closed it is probable there will be an amost entirely new force of attaches at the jail.

At the Bedside of Mrs. Soffel in the Butler General Hospital.

MRS. SOFFEL'S LAST MESSAGE.

Her Pitiful Words to Her Deserted and Disgraced Husband.

"Mamma, mamma, I didn t think you'd come."

Great, pitiful tears rolled down the white, pain-drawn cheeks of Mrs Soffel as Superintendent Cook, of the Butler Hospital, ushered into the room Mrs. Katherine Dietrich, stepmother of the dying woman

The little hospital on the hill never saw a sadder half-hour than when an erring daughter, wife and mother, wounded unto death, talked of her past with the only mother she has ever known. Mrs. Dietrich came from the room looking ten years older, and hurried from the hospital to a fast train, bearing from the wounded wife the last message to her husband, the man she had wronged and ruined. The burden of that message was "Forgive"

Mrs. Soffel suffered great pain during the interview, and it is now understood that hope of saving her life was abandoned before the hospital people consented to allow her stepmother to enter Mrs Soffel refused food and nourishment of any kind during the night, and it was a serious question whether anything would have been retained by her stomach had she taken it. During the short talk, in which she laid

bare the sinful secrets of her late career to Mrs.
Dietrich, Mrs Soffel became so ill that the attending
physicians were obliged to adopt heroic measures with
her

Mrs Dietrich believed she was dying, and fell on
her knees beside the little white bed on which the
wounded woman lay

Mrs Soffel was seized with a fit of coughing, and
by the time she recovered Mrs Dietrich, too, recovered
her composure, but her face was drawn and gray
Mrs Soffel cried softly and weakly as she raised one
arm, an arm on which there is a suspicious-looking
wound, and motioned for her stepmother to come
closer Superintendent Cook stepped back, as did all
in attendance, leaving them alone All felt, in some
ill-defined way, that it was the last message of an
erring wife to a wronged husband. Mrs Dietrich
leaned over the bed, her tears falling on that pale face,
and heard a few words. She nodded, and soon the
last farewell was said

It is known she seeks reconciliation with her husband, but he repels any such idea Her endeavor to
secure the services of Attorney W. A. Blakeley is a
significant fact Mr. Blakeley is a personal friend
of Mr Soffel, and he said that he would do all in
his power to help the Warden He left for Butler
to see Mrs Soffel The father of Mrs Soffel will
do all in his power to assist his erring daughter. "No,
never There will be no reconciliation between myself and wife," said Mr Soffel, in speaking of the
matter "Our marriage ties were severed when the
woman left my home, therefore, we will both seek
different walks in life."

LAST HOURS OF THE BIDDLES.

**Their Dying Confessions to Priest and Clergyman.
They Admitted All, but their Exact Words
will Never be Revealed.**

The Rev Father Daniel S Walsh, rector of St. Paul's Roman Catholic Church, who administered the last rites of the Church to the dying convicts, says: " Besides the statements given out by the Biddle boys to the newspapers and officers of Butler county, both ' Ed ' and ' Jack ' Biddle made confessions to me. ' Ed's ' was made on Friday night, there was no one present by myself John was lying in the next cell ' Jack ' did not confess until later. Their confessions were full and complete in every particular, and they will never be revealed

" While I was ministering to them almost every hour after they were brought to jail, they denied positively that they killed Grocer Kahney on Mount Washington, and Edward told me in the most emphatic terms that he did not shoot Detective Patrick Fitzgerald

" John also gave me a full account of their movements from Perryville through to Butler county to the spot where they were captured He did not, however, fill in the missing link and tell where they spent Thursday, and the name of the family which

81

protected them. The more I tried to elicit this from him the more he shunned the subject.

"They died like dogs, literally riddled with bullets, and someone should be held responsible for inhuman action in shooting them when entirely helpless, unarmed and unable to make the slightest defense or resistance

] "According to their statements I must judge them both innocent These were given without solicitation, and always were the same They had a sense of fear, and were fully cognizant of their condition, and I feel quite sure they did not pass into the great beyond with a lie on their lips·

The Rev. S M Kountz, pastor of the First English Lutheran Church, said recently.

"I visited the Biddles in their cell. 'Ed' was in a semi-conscious state at the time I placed my hand on his forehead, and he opened his eyes 'Jack' was perfectly conscious, and the jailer introduced me to him and informed him I was a preacher The man called 'Jack' weakly raised his left hand and I grasped it He had no strength, and it was plain for me to see his life was fast ebbing away

"He said: 'So you are a minister. I hope God may bless you. This is a hard, hard world to live in, as we have so found it'

"I replied: 'It is largely as you make it. How do you feel?'

"'I am dying,' he replied.

"Yes, I see you have not long to live; and you had better make peace with your Maker.'

"'I have already done so,' he said, 'I am growing constantly weaker, and I want to die. I'll be much better off.'

"At this point our conversation was interrupted by the arrival of the Rev. Father Walsh, and I withdrew to allow him to minister to 'Jack' Before I left the jail, however, I bade him good-bye, and he said 'This is the last time you ll ever see me alive, and I repeat, I hope God will bless you'

"As to whether I believe the Biddles guilty or innocent of the crimes charged to them I cannot definitely decide

"When the Biddles were brought here to jail on Friday night I was in the Sheriff's residence, and I must say the actions of Detective Charles McGovern were most scandalous The actions of Detectives Roach and Swinehart showed they were cool and collected and men entirely worthy of the office they fill"

ED. BIDDLE'S DYING CONFESSION.

**Blames the Zeber's Woman for the Murder and
Tries to Shield Mrs. Soffel, whom He Says
He Induced to do all She Did.**

On his deathbed in the jail hospital at Butler Ed
Biddle told the story of the crime, and placed all the
blame on the Zebers woman   He said Jennie Zebers,
of Milwaukee, Wis , first lived with Walter Dorman
She met him in Detroit, where she had been doing
sketches in small theaters in the Michigan lumber
regions   Dorman's home is in Cleveland.   He was
the mechanic of the Biddle gang

They began working in Pittsburg in January, 1901,
and a quick succession of crimes took place   It is
not known that the girls — the other was Jessie Bodine, from Pueblo, Col , who lived with Edward Biddle
— knew how the men made their living   But they
soon began accompanying them during their daylight
investigations

The burglaries were numerous and daring, and the
police could find no clews

After the capture of the Biddles, Dorman and the
two women, many came forward and identified the
quintet as having been noticed where robberies occurred.

The men used to take the women as though house-hunting. Walter Dorman was taken by surprise at his boarding-house Jennie Zebers was in the room when the detectives broke in, and both tried to get at revolvers

They succeeded, and Detective Fitzpatrick was shot and killed The dying man denied he shot Mrs Soffel, as had been alleged, and said she was shot by one of the deputy sheriffs and detectives who were firing a fusilade of bullets at the flying sleigh He calmly admitted he had made love to Mrs Soffel, not because he cared for her particularly, but because he wanted to use her as a means of escape He told in detail how he worked on her feelings and sympathy until she consented to the desperate resort of releasing them. It was she who furnished the saws with which they cut the bars, and afterwards gave them the revolvers with which to defend themselves At the last moment she begged to go with them Ed tried to dissuade her from so foolish a course, but she was obdurate, and he had no heart to leave her behind The rest is too well known to need further description.

With almost his last breath the dying bandit expressed his sympathy for the woman whom he had lured into such an awful scrape, and expressed the hope she would get out of it all right He admitted her devotion to them in their hour of direst need of a friend, had won their esteem, and that, bad as they were, they could but appreciate it and take her away with them They had not the heart to desert her, and with almost his last breath he sent her a message of condolence.

DEATH OF THE BIDDLES.

They Expired in Agony from their Many Wounds, while Mrs. Soffel Pleaded to See Them Once More Before They Died.

The death of the brothers Ed and John, as they lay side by side in the Butler County Jail, was pathetic, despite their crimes   As they lay gasping for breath, yet praying that death would soon end their agony, Mrs Soffel, who had given all for them, was in another portion of the prison, suffering from her wound terribly, but forgetting all her pain in her love for the wounded Ed   Piteously she begged to see him, and when a deaf ear was turned to her pleading her grief was heart-rending

The marvel is that men so shot to pieces should have survived as long as they   " Ed " Biddle had three wounds through his body, two of them near his heart. His brother, John, was simply riddled with Winchester and pistol balls   Besides this, he had two wounds, self-inflicted, in the mouth   He had five wounds in the body, and ten in his right arm

The woman's wound is in the breast   It was supposed that her corset steels had so deflected the course of the bullet that it had not penetrated the breast cavity.

86

The two men lay in adjoining cells in the Butler Jail, grimly facing death, and death came not easily. Both of them were anxious to die, and it is now certain that they and the woman formed a pact to kill themselves in the event of capture being certain

All three of them tried to abide by the pact   John Biddle, when he was already bleeding from a dozen wounds, put the muzzle of his pistol between his lips and was able to fire twice   His brother shot himself close to the heart

While the wounded murderers were on the verge of death the Sheriffs of Butler county and those from Pittsburg were fighting for the glory of the bloody capture and the $5,000 reward which was offered in Pittsburg for the retaking of the Biddles

The struggle for the blood money is bitter, and has already twice lined up the opposing officers with guns in their hands

The Butler county authorities said the prisoners were theirs, and lodged complaints of assault against the dying men as a warrant for holding them   The Pittsburg men said the Biddles should go back to Pittsburg   The first clash of these opposing forces came when Sheriff Hoon, of Butler, ordered the jail cleared of everybody save the local officers   This order included the Pittsburg men, and two of them drew their weapons and refused to go

Up to this time the jail had been like a booth at a fair   Every friend of every officer who had access to the jail was permitted to come in and stare at the two notorious criminals who were gasping for breath and writhing on their cots

Both posses, that from Pittsburg and that from Butler, were in at the fight near Prospect, and it is probable that ultimately the reward will be divided between them, but just now the Pittsburg detectives are insisting that the Biddles had surrendered to them before the Butler crowd reached them, a contention that is denied by the Butler officials and particularly by Deputy Sheriff Hoon, the son of the Sheriff, who says that, while Detective McGovern fired the first shot, the bullet that finally brought down "Ed" Biddle came from his revolver

Within fifteen minutes a crowd of three hundred men gathered at the jail door, most of them with guns in their hands, determined to resist any effort to take the murderers back to where the gallows awaited them

When the absurd rumor had been exploded, the crowd withdrew. Meanwhile the Biddles inside both seemed on the very threshold of death The doctors were injecting nitroglycerin, and were barely able to keep them breathing When it became evident that the Biddels were both likely to die soon, they were asked if there was anything that they wished done, or any last request they cared to make

"Ed ' Biddle whispered that he would like to see his brother, and John was carried into the cell, and they were laid side by side, while the crowd of officers watched their farewell

The two murderers were even sentimental as they bade each other good-by, but neither one of them said a word at that time about the woman who was at that moment in the hospital begging for a last sight of the man for whom she cast away husband, home, children, and for whom she dared hunger, exposure, fatigue, and finally death.

"Let me see 'Ed' just once, then I am ready to die," she repeated over and over in the hospital.

"I am all in, Jack," said "Ed" Biddle, as they laid his brother beside him, "good-bye, old man, we have pulled together, and I guess it's all right"

Jack Biddle took "'Ed's" hand, and from his mutilated throat came words of farewell The situation and their weakness brought them to the verge of delirium several times during the interview, and they talked to each other of their boyhood days, brokenly and wanderingly, and finally "Ed" Biddle asked his brother if he remembered their mother

A murmur of assent came from Jack

"I never loved anybody but mother," said "Ed"

It is doubtful if either of them knew what they were saying Jack was roused from a stupor into which he seemed to be falling, and bade his brother good-bye He also looked up at Mrs Hoon, the wife of the Sheriff, who had come into the cell, and quite clearly said good-bye to her His brother had fallen into a delirium, and the doctors were working on him as they carried John back to his own cell

"Ed" Biddle bled internally, at intervals he was racked with convulsions His brother was in an equally bad condition, and, in addition, suffered horribly One or two of the bullets that pierced his body tore his stomach and intestines

They died within an hour of each other Ed's end came first, and John's soon followed.

BENEATH THE SOD.

The Last Resting Place of the Biddles in Calvary Cemetary. As They had Lived and Sinned, Side by Side They Lie.

The curtain fell on one of life's saddest and most tragic scenes when the Biddles were laid beneath the sod It was their brother Harry's intention to bury them secretly, for fear their bodies would be stolen, but wise counsel prevailed and they were laid away in peaceful Calvary When the funeral profession reached the cemetery it wound its way along the serpentine roads to the place of burial — a bleak slope, snow-capped and swept by a bitter east wind — in the southern end of the grounds

A hundred friends of the dead criminals stood shivering about the open graves some time before the bodies arrived. The cold was intense, yet with bared heads and on bowed knees they joined in the burial service The two graves lie on a slope in the single interment plot in the southern end of the cemetery, and here side by side the Biddle boys were laid, separated by a narrow strip of clay

When the small procession stopped the pallbearers opened the hearse containing the remains of John Biddle, and carried them down the steep, slippery hillside to his grave. The flowers on the casket were removed, and the body lowered into the grave. They then brought the body of Edward and laid it beside his brother.

The Rev Father Miles Sweeney and a policeman stood at the foot of the graves while the bodies were being lowered, while other policemen escorted the remains from the hearse to the place of burial

When the two bodies were forever shut out from view Father Sweeney, clad in his clerical robe and wearing the purple stole across his left shoulder, raised his hands and pronounced the ritualistic Catholic service for the dead After the absolution had been read in low tones, the policemen standing beside Father Sweeney handed him two bottles of holy water, and these were emptied into the graves

Father Sweeney then bowed his head, and, kneeling in the snow, with the friends, pronounced the sad words of the Benediction Those about the grave joined in the responsive service, while many women wept

It was truly a most impressive scene, and never perhaps had a life's tragedy such a spectacular finale. The snow-covered cemetery, the yawning, open graves the shivering crowd, the gray-haired priest kneeling between the graves, all peace and quiet, the reverent spectators, the spotless snow, in such contrast with the sinning, the prison, the bloodshed of two days before.

McGOVERN'S CRUELTY.

A Detective is alleged to have Clubbed and Shot the
Dying Men. Also wanted to Shoot Mrs. Soffel.
Shocking Story of an Officer's Brutality.

In the story of the Biddle boys, shocking as it is,
there is not a more terrible chapter than that which
concerns Detective Charles McGovern, of the Pittsburg city force. As soon as the news of their escape
was made known, McGovern headed the party that
went in pursuit of them. After long trailing of them
his rage grew hourly, and one would have thought
the fleeing criminals had done him some personal injury by the bloodthirsty manner in which he followed
them. No savage lion with gleaming tusks and muzzle
reeking with blood ever followed the trail of his helpless prey any more savagely than did this cruel detective follow on the sleigh tracks of the two men
whose lives he craved. There was a large reward for
them dead or alive. He preferred to take them dead,
for the simple reason that in his failing heart he
dared not attempt to arrest them living. He knew
they were desperate, and that they would probably
never be taken alive. He feared for his own precious
life, and he wanted the reward. As soon as he came
in sight of them on the snow-covered road he began
firing at them with a Winchester rifle, little caring if
he killed the woman with them or not. Shot after
shot he fired, and then, reloading his sixteen-shooter,
he poured another volley into them after they had
fallen from the sleigh and were lying dying, with

93

their life blood crimsoning the immaculate snow he committed an act which would have sent another to the Penitentiary. As though they were serpents, he rushed at their writhing, agonized forms and shot them again and again as they lay dying With the butt of his rifle he beat them over the heads after he had fired into them every bullet his gun contained With a single blow he broke John Biddle's jaw, and then, like some wild animal, maddened by blood he raised his gun to shoot the screaming woman who had crouched behind the sleigh The hands of brother officers knocked the rifle barrel up, and others restrained him until his blodthirsty frenzy had abated Even those with whom he had pursued the fugitives upbraided him for his cowardice and brutality, and since then none of the officers will speak to him He is spoken of as "the tiger," and the consensus of opinion is that even the Biddles, desperate criminals that they were, were far more manly and humane than even he was

At the coroner's inquest the brutal detective was roundly scored for his cruelty, and a number of witnesses openly testified against him

Deputy Sheriff Rainey Hoon testified that McGovern struck Jack Biddle on the back of the head with the butt of his Winchester rfle when the latter was lying face down in the snow in the road and begging to be let die in peace

McGovern also, it is charged, shot one of the Biddles when the Deputy Sheriff was placing the handcuffs on him

All of the officers who were in the fight, except McGovern, who is in Pittsburg, and Robert Ray, who is ill, testified substantially to the same details as to the fight. When Detective John Roach, who was with the party, was asked about the shooting of the Biddles after they were down, and the striking of Jack with the butt of the gun, he asked to be excused from answering

He said he and McGovern had worked together and were good friends, and he would rather not go into that part of the story

Hoon said "McGovern and I walked up to them. They were both lying on their faces I walked up first, and McGovern swore at me for it I had a revolver in my hand, and had it loaded I walked up to them, and he walked up and hit Jack on the back of the head with the butt end of his Winchester when he was on his face Then I turned Ed over on his back I was the first to touch either of the men, and he was going to shoot them again He stepped back and shot Jack again after he was on the ground. I turned Ed over, and he said.

"'For God's sake don't shoot again — let me die'

"Mr. Holliday turned Jack over, and coaxed him not to abuse him, to let him die

'The slugs that entered the arms and side of Jack Biddle were from the shot fired by McGovern after he was lying face down on the snow, at close range"

Under the instructions of Coroner John L Jones an autopsy was held on both the Biddles The surgeons in charge were Drs McCurdy, Bricker and J. Clinton Atwell

The evidence secured by the autopsy bears out the statement that the Biddles intended to kill themselves rather than be taken alive, and that Ed succeeded in his attempt, while Jack failed, though his life was forfeited.

SADDEST PART OF THE TRAGEDY.

Pathetic Chapter in the Most Sensational of Modern Occurrences. The Hapless Warden who is Left to Suffer the Sequel all Alone Truly Deserving of Deepest Sympathy.

In Pittsburg the tumult of flight and alarms, the news of capture, and of wounds, of suffering and of death, left one man almost forgotten. He was Peter Soffel, keeper of the City Jail. For him, too. now all was in the past tense. His wife gone and, criminal, likely to be sent to serve time in the very prison he had presided over, for assisting State's convicts to escape, his position resigned, his home broken up, and his name disgraced. It was the least of the blows that had beaten him down that he had lost his wardenship. It was not much, but it was what he had of livelihood and profession, yet from the moment that he woke dazed and mentally wandering in his room in the keeper's quarters in the jail he resolved not to hold the post whereby he had been dishonored. What the future may hold for him he does not know, what the present holds, through no fault of his that men can see, is hourly anguish and bitter shame.

And there are the two misguided girls whom the dead bandits lured from their homes to enter upon a wild course of folly—one of them, Miss Bodine, hidden in a retreat where she is groping under kindly care for the parted threads of her life in the world of honest work, the other branded by the bandits in their final hour with the charge of complicity in the murder for which they were condemned

People tell you of the valor of these men, of the pains they took to consider and to shield the woman. How "true?" By using her, playing upon her emotions, turning her silly head with love talk and winning from her their freedom at the price of her shame? By permitting her to share their flight, their sufferings and their death battle, when they might indeed have shaken her off to a lucky death in the snow? Why, they might better have gone sensibly to the gallows than have accepted such a sacrifice and shown such " truth " and " faithfulness "

For a man can die but once, and hanging is not shame, but the deed that won it

Hanging? There are worse things. There lay the proof of it in pain and remorse in the hospital of Butler Shielded as the dead bandits were not from curious inquiry, cared for by every device known to science, she is being saved, healed, brought back to life

There is no doubt of it "A weaker woman would have died from cold and shock," she moaned "Oh, God, if I could die! If I could only die! Just one inch more to the right, just one little inch, and I wouldn't have to bear it all alone." And she traced with tremulous finger the course of the bullet that did not kill Then the fever took her, and with the labored breath of the pneumonia patient she gasped wildly: " I am so strong! I am so strong! A weaker woman would have died of cold and shock   Why can't I die?"

There are moments, though, when there dimly struggled in her mind the thought that a great theme and battle-ground for a possible retribution is centered in her sinning self   She babbled of a good God's mercy in letting her live, in giving her an opportunity to wipe out shame

"It had to be so," she said   "I had to stay to bear it.   God protect my unhappy husband and children!   God help me to live!   My soul will come through it purified"

What will she do?   Where can she hide that the story of her brief flight among the great stern realities of sin and passion and retribution will not find her out?   What new friends may she make, what old ones regain?   How repair the wrong, how live so as to repay with her weak woman's wit the great mischief she has wrought?   Or, will she soon despair once more of striving and with surer aim strike at her own life that she can no longer endure in daily torture and in hourly shame?

End of one story and beginning of another   And such a story!   Fraught with every element of concentrated horror, tense with the strongest dramatic suspense   How will the tangled plot unravel itself?

Who can tell even the story of her mental struggles and tortures in the past three months?   Edward Biddle's long letter, picked up in the snow outside the jail, revealed only the machinery of the plot   What it cannot tell, what will seem to Kate Soffel herself some day like an unbelievable nightmare is how she was won to leave her husband, whom she honored, and the children that she loved   Here is the unfath-

omable mystery of a woman's heart that lifts the tale
of it far out of the level of sordid crime and common-
place evil-doing   The Biddles are gone, judged, meas-
ured, their story told

The poor, misguided woman remains! In the hospital, guarded as a culprit under arrest by stalwart
policemen, who sit at the door of her room day and
night, waiting until she has recovered sufficiently to
allow of the taking her off to prison, she lay alone
and miserable, awaiting what Fate had in store for
her   It may be a term of years behind prison bars
She prays for death   She has nothing to live for
It would be sweet relief   Her story is yet to be told
Who shall write the story of Kate Soffel?

THE DETECTIVES' STORY.

Details of the Fight Told by the Men who Sent the Biddles Into Eternity.

The story of the fight has been told from the fugitives' side. Equally interesting is the story from the lips of the men whose deadly fire sent the Biddles into eternity. The most interesting version of it is given by J. Rainey Hoon, a son of Sheriff Hoon, and himself a deputy. It is as follows:

"I want to say in the beginning that it was our lives or theirs, and we did our duty. I feel no sorrow for the Biddles, for they were the men. For Mrs Soffel I do feel sorry, for she was only a foolish woman after all. And we did not shoot her. The wound in her breast was caused by herself.

"When we turned around from Mount Chestnut we traveled along a lonely road for about three miles. The snow was piled up high on either side. There were no fences either to the right or to the left. It was already growing a little dark, but it was still light enough to see a good distance ahead.

"My sleigh, containing McGovern, Roach and myself, was still in the lead, and we were driving rapidly. Perhaps a hundred yards ahead of us there was a crown in the road. What was beyond it we could not see, but as we drove on, whipping our

99

horses, we saw grow up over the brow of the rise a one-horse sleigh As the horse came fuller into view we could see three figures in the old-fashioned sleigh Thy were those of two men and a woman

"'There they are!' said McGovern

"As the sleigh came on the detectives recognized the Biddles There was a whispering between the men and we could see them shuffling about We knew they were getting their weapons ready So were we Ed Biddle sat on the right, he was driving John Biddle sat on the left, and Mrs Soffel was in the middle

"Fifty yards, forty yards, thirty yards, and then twenty yards That was all the space between us I'm telling this slowly, but there was a fearful swiftness about the way things moved out there on that road

' At ten yards Ed Biddle pulled up the horse He handed the reins to the woman, and she took them as though he were just stepping out to get a cigar Then he reached down and grabbed something that lay at the foot of the sleigh on the outside of the robe When he straightened up we straightened up we saw it was a shotgun

"He jumped out John Biddle, with drawn revolver, sprang out on the other side The woman still sat on the seat, holding the reins We, too, had leaped into the road The sleigh behind us had come up with a rush, on seeing that a fight was imminent

"Surrender or we will kill you, and that woman will be hurt!" I shouted, with the hope that regard for the woman who had tried so hard to save them would make them turn back at the last minute

"'Go to ——!'" the brothers shouted, and Ed Biddle raised his shotgun. He pulled the trigger and the load scattered down the road and whistled past our ears

"That was the opening shot of the battle John Biddle, on the other side of the sleigh, began pumping lead at us from his revolver Two rifles in our party answered the fire, and then we all joined in with our revolvers It rained bullets for a moment I could hear them singing past my ears and the fusillade sounded as though we were on the firing line of an army

"It couldn't have been more than thirty seconds when Ed Biddle, who had thrown aside his shotgun and was using his six-shooter, fell on his face

"Mrs Soffel had kept her eyes on him as she sat there holding the reins When she saw Ed fall she seemed to realize that her lover must be captured, and she dropped the reins The horse began to prance and jumped out. She grabbed a revolver and began to shoot

"'Kill 'em, Jack,' she screamed

"She stood straight up in the sleigh, and the horse jumped back and forth at each report, throwing her down on the seat She stood up again, and, at that instant, Jack Biddle fell With a terrible scream the woman began to denounce us The horse plunged down the embankment to the left of the road Mrs Soffel, standing up and looking back, saw the two brothers in the road with the bloody snow all about them We were all rushing up to seize them, and she knew it was the end

"There was one shot left in her revolver, and she turned it on herself Hiding her eyes with her free hand, she fired, and toppled over into the bottom of the sleigh "

TRAILED BY 'PHONE.

Remarkable Story of the Pursuit by Telephone and and Telegraph Until the Detectives Reached Butler.

The fate of the Biddles was in the hands of the Pittsburg police early on the morning after their escape Superintendent of Police McAleese and Superintendent of Detectives Demmel, with their ears to telephone receivers, practically followed the murderers and their companion for mile after mile as they drove through the snow of Butler county It was only a question how quickly detectives could get 'o Butler or some point on the hot trail for the end of the chase

Early in the day officers of the Forest Oil Company and the National Transit Company received reports from along their lines positively identifying a party on the Butler plank road as the Biddles and Mrs Soffel Before 7 o'clock the chase had actually begun

Superintendents McAleese and Demmel have never had a similar experience in their careers as police officers They received assistance of inestimable value from several sources, and have given full credit J. G Splane, Common Councilman from the Thirteenth Ward, and manager of the Forest Oil Company, sat with the officials in the private office of the Superintendent of Police and directed the pursuit until Detectives John Roach, Charles McGovern and Albert Swinehart reached Butler

Practically the chase started in earnest from Cooperstown In reality the fugitives were tracked from Perrysville The information to the police was that the party left there in the stolen sleigh, a new one, with a stolen white-faced horse, about 1 o clock in the morning From Perrysville they took to the plank road, passing through Talley Cavey, the village of Bakerstown (not the railroad station), and on to Cooperstown, where they arrived about seven o clock.

At Cooperstown the party had the horse fed and got breakfast at the house of J A Snyder, a liveryman The rig and the party attracted much attention Mrs Soffel was dressed in handsome clothes, with a white fascinator about her head She wore a light raglan coat, and there were diamonds on her fingers For three-quarters of an hour the Biddles remained there, watchful, uncommunicative, and restless. One of the Biddles remained outside of the house, on guard, and Mrs. Soffel and the other Biddle were eating

To several who inquired, after suspicion had been aroused, the Biddles said they were on their way to visit an aunt who lived near the plank road between Glade Mill and Butler But the party was not equipped for such a journey The horse had already apparently traveled some distance There were no blankets or robes in the sleigh The harness was an unusual one for country driving, and there were no bells on the horse

F. A. Holliday, gauger for the National Transit Company at Butler, who was among the little crowd at Cooperstown, soon became convinced that the strangers were lying Then the features of the men and the woman impressed themselves upon him, and he believed they were none other than the Biddles and Mrs Soffel He wanted to pursue at once, but his companions were slow to share his beliefs

Holliday reported to A B Gregory, Superintendent of the Forest Oil Company Gregory got into communication with the Butler and Pittsburg offices, and Councilman Splane soon received a detailed description of the party, which was so strikingly accurate that he reported to Superintendent McAleese The Pittsburg police, with a description of the stolen horse and sleigh, at once concluded that they had the right track, and plans were laid to hold it until armed detectives could be rushed into Butler county by train

Splane held the private telephone wires at the service of the police In a few minutes Holliday had been dispatched from Cooperstown to follow the Biddles From that time the police had accurate information every half hour or so from points along the line, showing exactly what progress was being made by the fugitives

The Biddles, although nervous at Cooperstown, do not appear to have taken any serious alarm But they were afraid to pass through Butler, and evidently did not know the roads in that territory well enough to keep off the main traveled highways

Holliday drove on to Butler Just before entering the town the Biddles had taken to side streets and cut into a road leading to the east Holliday went into Butler and quickly organized a posse All the stops were reported to police headquarters. At Sutton's store it was known the Biddles had stopped for a few minutes. They had warmed themselves at the stove in the store, and had watered the horse. One of the Biddles asked the storekeeper for a box of shoe blacking.

While Holliday was scouting ahead Splane was preparing another move to assist the police. J. A. Snyder, the Cooperstown liveryman, who had fed the fugitives in the morning, and who could be depended upon to recognize them and their team, was sent in a sleigh with a powerful pair of horses to follow Holliday and meet the Pittsburg detectives at Butler.

Superintendents McAleese and Demmel, in the meantime, had given instructions to Detectives Roach, McGovern and Swinehart. It was found that there was no train to Butler before one o'clock. The necessary delay of several hours for a time threatened to prolong the chase indefinitely, but the telephone wires were held and the latest reports indicated that the Biddles had seemingly lost their way, that their horse was badly fagged, and that the whole country-side about Butler was aroused and on watch for the stolen rig and its desperate occupants.

" Shoot. Don't give them a chance to open on you ; and, above all things, don't give them any show of getting away. If they fire, shoot to kill."

These were the instructions to the detectives. Armed with Winchester rifles and a brace of heavy revolvers each, they reached Butler in time to join a new posse. Splane's reports were that Holliday and his posse, after riding out to the east for about eight miles, concluded the Biddles had doubled somewhere, and they returned to Butler On the outskirts of the town they found where the quarry had turned north.

Then the police received reports that the Biddles had stopped at a store just north of Butler. Holliday estimated that when he left the track and went to Butler he was about one hour behind the chase The late reports indicated that not much had been lost by the long ride east toward Petrolia and the Allegheny River He and his posse also found, on returning to Butler, that Snyder was there and that the Pittsburg detectives had just arrived and were ready to renew the pursuit

North and west of Butler, Spiane's telephone service did not reach points along the line of the flight, but it kept an open line of communication with Butler and the Pittsburg police were well informed of the movements up to within a short time of the first reports that the quarry had been run down that it had fought, and had been shot down by the Pittsburg detectives.

DID SHE SIN ?

Mrs. Soffel Expresses Repentance for Her Folly, and Claims She is Still a Virtuous Wife.

Aside from her criminal offense of releasing State's prisoners and aiding them to escape, her desertion of her husband, children and home, and flight with her self-confessed lover, Ed Biddle, Mrs Soffel still contends she is guiltless of any criminal wrongdoing with him   In the Butler Hospital she said to Assistant District Attorney Robb

"I am not a bad woman, Mr Robb," sobbed the patient   "I know how much I am blamed in the eyes of the world. I know that I have been charged with a crime against the State. My guilt or innocence will in time be established, but what I want you to understand is that I have never sinned

' I know how my husband must feel over what has transpired, and I am anxious to save him as much suffering in the future as I can, as some slight atonement   I do not want to go back to Allegheny county to be tried   My husband has suffered far too much through me already   The publicity which the case would receive by being tried in Pittsburg would only humiliate him the more   Can you not arrange it so that the case could be taken to some place far from Pittsburg, where my husband and myself are not so well known?"

There were tears in her eyes and a pathetic pleading in her voice. The answer she received brought little comfort. Mr Robb could make no promise. He said that such things are done sometimes, where a doubt exists that a defendant may not receive justice. He did not tell the woman so, but his language indicated that changes of venue are seldom secured in order to accommodate the whims of a person. Mrs. Soffel, pleading for a change of venue, indicates that repentance has come.

Mr. Robb told the suffering woman that he is a friend of her husband, and would go to a great length to help him in his trouble, but that he could give her no assurance that her request would be granted. This reference of Mrs. Soffel to her husband is the most extended she has made since her capture. Heretofore she seemed anxious to avoid speaking of him, but her trouble seemed preying on her mind even more than usual, and she unburdened herself completely.

In contradiction of her claims of chastity, as she alleged, is the statement that when they stopped at the little roadside inn for food for themselves and horse, Ed Biddle and Mrs Soffel, who passed as man and wife, went upstairs to a room together and remained there for some time, while Jack Biddle waited downstairs. That was in all probability when Mrs Soffel fell, and her husband will use the hotelkeeper as a witness in his divorce proceedings.

MRS. SOFFEL NOT ALONE.

If Her Husband Gets a Divorce there are Men who would Marry Her.

Mrs. Soffel is not alone, despite her sinning, and there are men who would marry her tomorrow if she was free and divorced. They admire her pluck and devotion. She might in turn betray them, but they would take chances willingly on that.

Although one would naturally think that the path of crime was the least likely of all to lead to the altar, it is a very remarkable thing that some of the most notorious criminals known have been simply inundated with offers of marriage from unknown sympathizers and admirers In fact, such is the fascination of crime to persons of a certain class that it is almost safe to say that the more brutal and heartless the criminal the better are his or her matrimonial chances

Neil Cream, the famous, or rather infamous poisoner; Deeming, the Australian wife-killer, Fauntleroy and many others of the greatest scoundrels of our time, might have been married over and over again if Justice had not substituted the halter for the altar, and for a woman to commit a crime, especially if she be at all good looking, is to awaken tender emotions in many a manly breast.

A few years ago, when a certain young man of rank was charged with a particularly heartless crime, at least a score of silly women promptly fell head over heels in love with him and inundated his solicitors with messages of sympathy, offers of financial help, and of marriage

Every day of his trial some of them attended the court and exhausted every strategy to get a word with him, and when he was sentenced to five years' penal servitude, one woman, an absolute stranger to him, fainted in court

So infatuated was one of his lovers that she went to live in the neighborhood of the prison where he served his sentence, and was happy if she caught a glimpse of him on his way to the quarries Whether she married him or not ultimately cannot be said, but it certainly was not her fault if she didn't.

In another case which occurred at about the same time a young and pretty girl was charged with the manslaughter of her child under peculiarly sad conditions Her case excited wide sympathy, and at least a dozen men wrote to make her offers of marriage. After a long trial she was acquitted, and one of her numerous lovers, a man of some wealth, found a home for her, and at the end of six months led her to the altar This strangely united couple are now living on the Continent, and are very happy together.

ODD STORIES ABOUT BIDDLES.

A Few Random Items in Their Careers which are Extremely Interesting.

Had Edward Biddle failed in his plans to escape from the Allegheny County Jail, he was prepared to cheat the hangman, and, it is supposed, would have done so by poisoning himself In a strap which was taken as a souvenir from a garment he wore, by Thomas Redd, a strychnine pill, large enough to kill two men, was found by Redd's mother The pill was examined by Dr Shultis, who gave out the fore-going statement

The sentimental side of Ed Biddle's nature was forcibly recalled one night, when the dead criminal s clothing he wore when captured was searched for trinkets, letters or papers

In the vest pocket was a single violet, carefully wrapped in oil paper, with no marks about it to show whence it came It is believed to be the flower that the little daughter of Rev Mr. Foster, pastor of the Knoxville Methodist Episcopal Church, Pittsburg, sent to Ed when he was in the Allegheny County Jail, and concerning which he wrote the poem pub-lished in this book

A H Schroederer, a barber of 603 Ann street, Homestead, in closing up his books for the year, was reminded by an entry on them that a man named Edward Biddle worked for him one week, beginning March 17 and ending March 24, last year He distinctly remembers the young fellow, and said that his description in every way tallies with that of the outlaw

Schroederer said recently that Edward Biddle was a very good barber and unusually quick in making friends with customers For that reason he felt regret when, after a week of satisfactory service, Biddle said that he could work no longer and left During that same week there were eleven robberies in Homestead Nebo's hardware store was one of the heaviest losers, about one hundred and fifty dollars worth of revolvers and guns being stolen from it Several of these weapons were found in the Fulton street house at which Biddle was arrested afterward

Biddle left four razors, all apparently new, with Schroederer, and as they have never since been called for, the dead burglars estate is probably entitled to them unless a prior owner, from whom they were stolen, should put in a claim for them.

Wearing the garb of nuns, disguised as ministering angels of the Roman Catholic Church, the Biddles and Mrs Soffel hoped to make their escape. It was Mrs Soffel's plan, and the arrangement was that as soon as the trio had reached a place of temporary safety they were to don the black robes and veils as traveling Sisters of Mercy They had planned to make for some remote mining place in Canada, where they were to live together.

Ed Biddle told Mrs Soffel that he intended to give up his former nefarious trade and work in the mines with Jack This plan was made known to Dr Mc-Curdy Bricker at the Butler Hospital by Mrs Soffel, and was confirmed by Jack Biddle While Dr Bricker was attending the dispirited woman at the hospital he confided in him this plan of escape.

FATE PURSUES CRIMINALS.

Like a Nemesis it Trails the Evil-Doer to His Final Doom.

It is the inability of the shrewdest criminal to keep going without making a fatal mistake that detectives depend upon to catch them, said an old detective. Men with more brains than the Biddle boys, men higher up in the profession of burglary, have made mistakes just as they did, and lost their freedom or their lives thereby. It is nearly always drink, women or cards with criminals, and the officers watch the haunts of these fellows as closely as possible. With the Biddles it was a woman. I never expected them to try to take Mrs Softel with them. What I expected — and the reasonable thing for them to do — was to make an appointment to meet the woman somewhere, then never meet her. I had no idea they would be taken until they were arrested for some new crime. But they made the fatal mistake. They kept together and took the woman along, and they were immediately a mark for everyone who reads the papers.

But the Biddles were not clever burglars. They had not learned their profession. They were small housebreakers, and had not learned the first axiom of burglars who know their business — "Don't shoot if

114

you can possibly avoid it." The mere fact that they shot Grocer Kahney is evidence that they were not clever. All that was ever found on them was cheap stuff. They were not clever enough to burglarize a store or take any chance with the police They might have gone on in their small way for a long time if they had been clever enough to get out of the Kahney house without using a gun

Real, first-class burglars are practically of the past. Electricity has wiped them out Banks and business houses worth robbing are too well protected Not only burglar alarms are in the way, but far more difficult to overcome are the well-lighted streets of all cities

Consequently, the field for first-class burglars is narrowed down to the suburbs and to the small towns. How many years has it been since a real bank robbery has occurred? It can't be done any more. It has been so long since there have been any real opportunities that the expert burglar who could open any safe made are all dead, in prison or carzy None of the old experts are in the business, and no new crop has grown up. Electricity has done the work — has done more to rid the country of clever rouges than all the police of the world combined

Many people have foolish ideas of how to act if they discover a burglar in the house They think it is the part of a brave man to get out of bed and attempt to drive the burglar from the house The really proper thing to do is to cover up your head and don't let the thief know you heard him Let him get the $50 or $100 worth of plunder and get away as quietly as possible. That is not the act of a coward It is

115

a fool who attacks an armed burglar ready to shoot when he is in a corner.

A detective has said. ' If I were to walk out on the street and come face to face with a man badly wanted, and if he were to get the drop on me and order me to step back, I'd step back People might say I was a coward, but I'm not going up against an armed man without pretty nearly an even chance with him A criminal is only taking the chances that come to him in the way of business, and he is, or ought to be, cool and ready for whatever comes The average man in a case of this kind is taken by surprise. The burglar has a plan, and he hasn't. It's like an excited mob going up against an army of trained and disciplined men. The trained men get the best of it.

" There are lots of criminals who have never been caught, and never will be. Three members of the famous Blinkey Morgan gang in Ohio are still at large. There are scores like them. But they had to quit the business, for sooner or later the cleverest of them, if they keep at it, will make the fatal mistake, just as the Biddle boys did. It's the fate of the habitual criminal."

HARRY BIDDLE'S SACRIFICE.

Innocent Man has Nearly Beggared Himself to Defend and Bury His Erring Brothers.

Weighted down with a sorrow too deep to describe, and burdened with responsibility, poor Harry Biddle, of Pittsburg, the best of them all, has been unfailing in his devotion to them. The story of the innocent brother's love forms still another romance in this most remarkable series of romances. There have been many dramatic features connected with the lives of the dead brothers, but none more filled with elements of human interest than the sacrifices made by Harry Biddle and his faithful wife for them. Willing to give up everything to aid the erring ones, they express themselves glad now that all is over.

Now that all is over and the tension ended, Harry Biddle and his wife are beginning to realize the tremendous strain that they have been under during the past ten months According to the statements of both, their anxiety and worry have been terrible. They have practically beggared themselves and children in order to help Ed and Jack

The extent of the sacrifices made by Harry Biddle and his wife are not known to the public When it was found that funds were necessary for the defense of the brothers, Harry at once sold his interest in the Hope Restaurant, on Liberty street, and cheerfully gave up the amount realized from the sale. In addition to this he had a little money saved, and this soon followed. Then more money was needed. This was raised by placing a mortgage on the furniture contained in the little home at No. 98 Knox avenue The amount realized was small, but aided in the fight for life. A short time later Mrs Biddle sold her sealskin cloak and turned the money over to the lawyers Several other articles were converted into cash, and all went for the same purpose

The expense of the funeral had to be met Biddle had nothing except his daily earnings, yet he did not shrink from the additional burden placed on him and his wife's shoulders Mrs Biddle all in her power to aid her husband "They were Harry's brothers," she said, "and it was our duty to see that they received a decent burial Criminals though they undoubtedly were, we owed them a duty, and we paid it I never saw either Jack or Ed until, upon their arrival in Pittsburg, they came to our house. But my husband's wishes rule my will, and whatever he does will receive my sanction and support."

IMPLEMENTS OF THE ESCAPE.

The Saws and Pistols Used by the Biddles were Bought by Mrs. Soffel at McKeesport.

The saws and revolvers which assisted the Biddles to liberty were purchased at McKeesport, Pa, by Mrs. Soffel. The men who sold them to her will be the witnesses against her at her trial. They are now in the possession of District Attorney Haymaker   Ed Biddle upbraided the woman for getting saws that were useless, and advised her to go to McKeesport to make her purchases, where she could do so without exciting suspicion.   Mrs. Soffel followed the advice and went to McKeesport the next day

Mrs Soffel made the rounds of the McKeesport hardware stores   She inquired for " saws that would cut iron," and did not know of any name for them or what size she wanted.   Her manner was that of a person confused   In making her purchases she said: " Oh, I guess these will do "   At the store where she bought the revolver she said that her husband was away a great deal, and that she was afraid to remain at home unarmed   She bought no ammunition

The woman purchased three saws at the store of the Hartman Hardware and Supply Company, Fifth avenue, a block from the tea store.   John Smith, a clerk, says she asked him whether he had any saws that would "cut iron" He asked her if she wanted any particular brand, and she replied, "No" He then asked her what size she wanted and she appeared confused, telling him that she supposed they were all alike, and that her husband had not told her what size to get The clerk then showed her two of three sizes of hack saws, and after a superficial inspection the woman selected one and said· "Oh, I guess this will do Give me three"

Evidently the woman did not wish to invite suspicion by asking for a revolver at the same store, as she went farther out Fifth avenue to a branch store of the Hartman Company, where a clerk sold her a revolver.

THE SIGNAL CODE.

Clever Arrangement by which Mrs. Soffel and the Biddles Communicated with Each Other.

The code discovered was made up by Ed Biddle, and was a variation of the methods used by criminals in jails and penitentiaries where the cell bars are rapped by pipes to sound a code. The code was for use only between Murderers' Row and the windows of the Warden's residence, directly opposite, and was intended to obviate the necessity of frequent visits of Mrs Soffel to the prisoners' cells, which the Biddles feared might lead to detection

The entire alphabet was contained in that part of the body visible above the sill of the window of the Warden's residence, or from the head to the hips. Whenever Mrs Soffel pointed to her forehead Ed Biddle knew that she was spelling the letter A One of the eyes was B, and another C The nose was D, the mouth E, the chin F, and the ears G and H The shoulders, elbows, breasts and either hip meant certain other letters of the alphabet. Clasping both hands in front meant a period, and that it was the completion of a sentence

The code was taught to Mrs. Soffel by her prisoner-lover, and he made her a copy to study in her room, lest she should forget. It is suspected that either she tore the code paper into fragments when she was making her last hasty toilet preparatory to leaving the prison, or else the work was done by someone who remained behind and who had knowledge of the secrets of the unfortunate woman

The letter and code will be used in the prosecution of Mrs Soffel

The story now develops that Reynolds discovered Keeper Dietrich intently watching something one evening, and he asked him what it was

The custom of prisoners to strike matches and the possibility of seeing their reflection in the jail windows did not appear to him as unusual, although the discovery later of the desire of Ed Biddle to get as many matches as possible forced obvious conclusions upon him

Mrs Frances A. Burns, matron at the jail, says that Mrs Soffel visited the cells of the Biddles on several occasions immediately before the escape, remaining at the cells several hours each visit. Mr. Dietrich was on duty at the time. It is declared by the guards that the Biddles sawed the bars of their cells on those evenings, and that Mrs. Soffel warned the prisoners of the approach of the guards, who seldom went near the " Queen of the Jail," as Mrs. Soffel was affectionately called by prisoners and guards, was engaged in her conversations. They declare that the bars were not sawed previous to that, as was stated to have been the case in the letter found on Ed Biddle.

Mrs. Soffel was in the habit of saving wads of chewing gum and of sticking them, after the manner of seminary girls, on the backs of photographs.

Warden Soffel discovered a number of these wads on the back of a photograph of Mrs Soffel that he desired to lend to a friend, and he laughed at the peculiar habit of his wife It was these wads of gum that were used in cementing temporarily the sawed ends of the bars of the Biddle cells.

A PHILOSOPHICAL ARGUMENT.

The Case Reviewed and Analized in a Light which Shows Its Many Phases.

There are various ways in which that astonishing and horrible Biddle affair in Pennsylvania can be looked at

The artist is privileged to put aside all other considerations in his appreciation of the strong play of human passions and the terrific dramatic situations. Two brothers, professional criminals, are awaiting in prison their death by the rope for murder One of them wins the love of the warden's wife She supplies them with saws and pistols They break from their cell, fight and conquer the guard, and gain their liberty. The woman goes with them The price of her assistance is their consent to that. The three wander up and down the snow-covered country roads by night and day in a stolen sleigh. The men know that by burdening themselves with the infatuated creature to whom they owe their chance of escaping the halter they are surely throwing that chance away. But they will not break faith with her The officers appear There is a battle on the highway The men are shot, and the woman shoots herself. Both the men die, glad that they had cheated the rope, and the woman lies at the hospital at the point of death from her wounds and exposure to the bitter weather while with her criminal yet loyal lover   All this is melodrama of the most lurid kind, ready-made for the playwright   Poets and sentimental persons may well heave the sigh of sensibility over Mrs Soffel, as one who held the world well lost for love   They may also give their admiration to the two desperadoes for the chivalry that bound them to their pledge not to part company with her who for the sake of one had sacrificed all that a woman should value, and was prepared to die with them

People who are neither artists nor poets nor sentimentalists will decide that the persons concerned in this strangely stated tragedy who deserve greatest sympathy are the Warden and his children

No wonder that the Warden, foully betrayed as a husband, and basely tricked as an officer, by the wife, has thrown up his office and given way to agonies of shame and fury. No wonder he groans for the future of his boys and girls, whose mother's sin will follow and oppress them through life   Who can tell what fell influence that frightful knowledge of the wickedness of one who naturally should possess their deepest love and reverence will have upon their plastic young characters?

The woman is, nevertheless, entitled to pity; but that father, who, as deputy warden, carried verses from the lover in the scaffold's shadow to his own daughter, knowing that she was mad for the felon, isn't he appalling?

The sympathetic may in their several ways make heroes of the Biddles and a heroine of Mrs Soffel, but the great sympathy of balanced people will go out to the husband and father, half-mad in his misery, and to the hapless children of so reckless a mother.

It was hoped that before these words appeared in print the woman herself would have passed into the presence of the only One who can understand her — the God who created her

There is no place left upon earth for her. Without any personal acquaintance or knowledge of the woman's mental make-up, habits of thought or intimate life, it is impossible to more than generalize in suppositions regarding the causes which led to her act

First of all, she was at a period of life when the average woman is most restless and inclined to sentimental folly

This is not generally conceded to be a fact, but a little observation will prove the statement to be true It is the woman from thirty-five to fifty who most frequently figures in the divorce courts, not the girl in her teens or twenties

Look at our ultra-fashionable society, and you will find that the most sensational divorce cases have mature women in the leading rôles

Where a woman is deeply religious by nature she not infrequently cheats herself into the idea that dangerous attachments are actuated by her highest and holiest impulses

Sympathy in the average woman is a morbid sentiment, and neither reason nor judgment guides its expression as a rule.

It is, like her passions, closely allied to the sentiment in her nature, and in the crude woman sentiment is sentimentality.

Many such women are indifferent wives and mothers until their husbands or children fall ill or in dis-

grace, when they are all devotion The husband of
such a wife once said that it paid him to be sick, as
that was the only time he found any affection in his
wife, who was called an angel of mercy at all the sick-
beds in the neighborhood

She devoted herself to invalids lunatics and criminals The healthy, normal and moral world contained little to interest her

It is very easy for such a woman to believe herself
a good Christian, and doubtless Mrs Soffel deceived
her own heart to the final decisive hour regarding
her interest in the magnetic criminal who had aroused
her sympathies, her sentimentality and her passions

Speaking from a general survey of humanity in this
respect, it is safe to say that Mrs Soffel had not read
an impassioned love-letter, or heard a romantic avowal
of love, for a decade or more

Most husbands drop that line of address after a year
or two of marriage, thinking the wife understands and
appreciates the affection and loyalty of a good man
and liberal provider

Far more susceptible to flattery and possessed of a
vanity more easily aroused than that of a young girl, is
the matron who hears for the first time in many years
romantic phrases of love from the lips of a man
younger than herself

Summing up the causes which led to this terrible
tragedy, one would say first of all that Mrs Soffel
was deeply sympathetic with the condemned men,
then that she became impressed with their innocence,
and anxious to save them from an ignominious death
Third, that she began to feel the physical magnetism
of a powerful personality such as the younger criminal
possessed ; and no woman can feel this influence with-

out the man is conscious of it.

Once conscious of what he had awakened, the condemned man began his love - making — and reason, honor, womanhood, wifely dignity and motherly pride went down before it

May God pity her and help all her victims to bear the burdens she has put upon them!

FINIS.

Since the commencement of this book Mrs. Soffel has been taken to Pittsburg, and was in jail there two hours. Then her aged father appeared and gave $5,000 bail for her appearance in court. She was then released, and he took her home with him

In the September, 1902, term of the Pittsburg Criminal Court, Judge Frazer sentenced Mrs. Soffel to two years in Western Penitentiary.

CPSIA information can be obtained at www.ICGtesting.com
Printed in the USA
LVOW03s0249070115

421829LV00025B/847/P